GOLF

Grand golf tournament by professional players: Eleven golfers pose on Leith golf links, Edinburgh, Scotland, 17 May 1867.

A STEP-BY-STEP GUIDE TO PLAYING BETTER GOLF

ROB BLUCK, TESSA PAUL

GOLF

A STEP-BY-STEP GUIDE TO PLAYING BETTER GOLF

ROB BLUCK, TESSA PAUL

Abbeydale Press

This edition is published by Abbeydale Press,
an imprint of Anness Publishing Ltd
Hermes House, 88–89 Blackfriars Road London SE1 8HA
tel. 020 7401 2077; fax 020 7633 9499

www.annesspublishing.com

Anness Publishing has a new picture agency outlet for images for
publishing, promotions or advertising. Please visit our website
www.practicalpictures.com for more information.

Produced for Anness Publishing Ltd by Editorial Developments,
Edgmond, Shropshire, England
Design by: Bacroom Design and Advertising
Index: Marie Lorimer Indexing Services

ETHICAL TRADING POLICY
Because of our ongoing ecological investment programme, you, as our customer,
can have the pleasure and reassurance of knowing that a tree is being cultivated on
your behalf to naturally replace the materials used to make the book you are holding.
For further information about this scheme, go to *www.annesspublishing.com/trees*

PUBLISHER'S NOTE
The author and publishers have made every effort to ensure that all instructions
contained within this book are accurate and safe, and cannot accept any legal
responsibility or liability for any resulting injury, damage or loss to persons or property
that may arise from following advice or instructions in this book, nor for any errors,
omissions or inaccuracies that may be made. Any use to which the recommendations,
ideas and techniques are put is at the reader's sole discretion and risk.

CONTENTS

Introduction

Anybody wanting to take up the game of golf would naturally want to be good at it. A younger person would probably fancy their chances of becoming a Tiger Woods, whilst a more mature person may lower their sights a little and be happy to be able to play the game with confidence and attain a healthy handicap.

Whatever your situation is, there is always room for improvement and like many other sports, the more time you spend practising, the better you should become. This section of the book is created to give the novice a helping hand on the first tricky rungs of how to play golf, brush up the skills of the average player and remind the good players that they may have picked up some bad habits!

Whichever category you fall into, there is bound to be a tip or two to help you improve your golf, be it just a small positional adjustment or a whole new approach.

We hope that the moves Rob Bluck, Professional at the Lilleshall Golf Club in Newport, Shropshire, England, has taken the time to demonstrate, will go some way to helping you improve your handicap.

Golf Swing

Driving

Long Irons

Fairway Metals

Hybrids

Mid Irons

Short Irons

Pitching

Chipping

Putting

Greenside Bunkers

Fairway Bunkers

Awkward Lies

Awkward Bunkers

Shape It

Golf Swing

The Aim

If you take a look at the great players you'll notice that they all go through a strict set-up routine. The majority of them start every golf shot from directly behind the ball. (1a,1b)

You can see that I have positioned myself directly behind the ball and in line with my intended target. From this position I can see where I want the golf ball to go and, more importantly, I can pick out my ball-to-target line.

The ball-to-target line is an imaginary line that runs from the golf ball to the intended target. I see so many golfers bypassing the alignment stage and then wondering why they are hitting shots here, there and everywhere. It's so important to aim correctly; if your aim is poor you will have to manipulate the golf club throughout the swing, resulting in inconsistent golf shots. Aiming towards a target that is so far away can be very difficult; I try and pick out a point approximately 12 inches in front of my golf ball. This point can be a piece of dirt, a different shade of grass, a leaf or anything that is clear to see.

In picture (2) you can see I have placed a tee peg in the ground. Please note that this is purely for tuition purposes as you cannot use an artificial device such as a tee peg to align your shots when playing golf.

Here you can see that I am carefully aligning my club face towards the target (3). Once I am happy with my aim I am going to place my feet and knees together with the golf ball in the centre of my shoes. It is now time to position my hands on the grip.

Get a grip

The golf grip is probably the most important stage of the set-up routine. It's the only part of your body that actually makes contact with the golf club, and the way you position your hands on the club will affect the flight and direction of your golf ball and will also affect the way you swing the golf club.

Think of the golf grip like this:

The left hand is the *gripping/positional hand*.

I like to refer to the left hand as the gripping hand because it's the main hand that will support the golf club through various stages of the golf swing. You'll often see golfers wearing a glove on their left hand (the gripping hand) to prevent the golf club from slipping during the key stages of the golf swing.

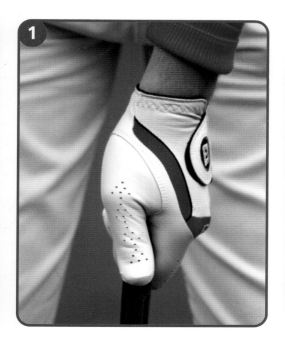  

(1) Notice how I have positioned my left hand on the golf club. You can see that two knuckles on the back of my left hand (not including the thumb joint) are visible; also notice how the hand is positioned slightly over to the right side of the golf grip (with thumb slightly on the right side of grip). You should see that a V-shape has formed between my thumb and forefinger (2). This V-shape is pointing to my right shoulder (3). The reason why I position the left hand like this is to enable the golf club to pass through various stages of the golf swing utilising my wrists correctly, without losing grip of the club, enabling me to maximise my power and accuracy.

Golf Swing

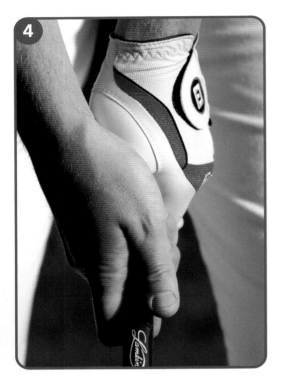

The right hand is the *hitting/releasing hand.*

In picture (4) you can see how my right hand has now joined the golf club. I am gripping the golf club through the fingers on my right hand. Gripping the club through the fingers will enable me to release the golf club correctly at the impact. In golfing terminology, releasing the golf club means the club head overtaking the hands, creating the snap or whip.

Think of it like throwing a ball; to throw a ball correctly you would hold it in your fingers not the palm of your hand, the reason being that you are able to release the ball better and therefore send it greater distances. The same applies when hitting a golf shot.

The forearms and hands rotate through the hitting area creating a whipping action, firing the golf ball great distances. Notice also how the V-shape on the right hand is pointing to my right shoulder. I am gripping the golf club in the middle two fingers of my right hand and there is no great pressure on my thumb or forefinger. Most importantly, the palm of my right hand is facing the target and is positioned square to the club face.

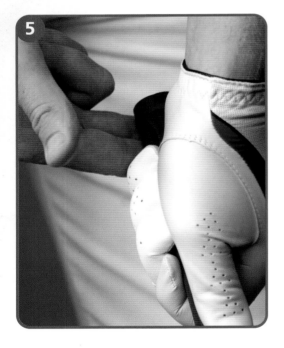

Where do I grip it?

I am often asked where I should position my hands, how high or how low? I have a really simple rule I tend to stick to. When hitting a full shot make sure you give yourself a two-finger gap at the top.

Notice how I have taken my right hand off the club and I am measuring the distance from the little finger of my left hand and the very top (butt) of the golf grip (5).

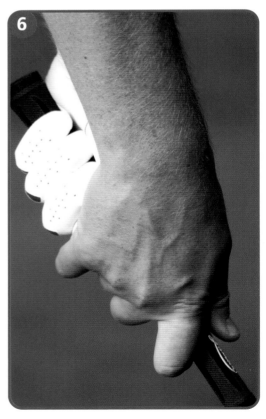

This is about perfect: you can see that the muscle pad on my left hand is supporting the very top (butt) of the golf grip (6).

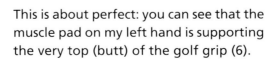

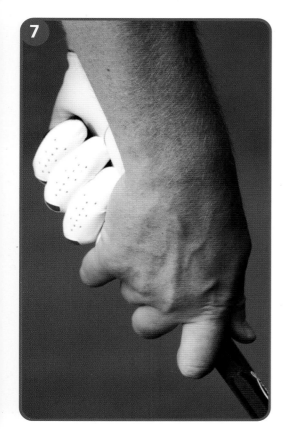

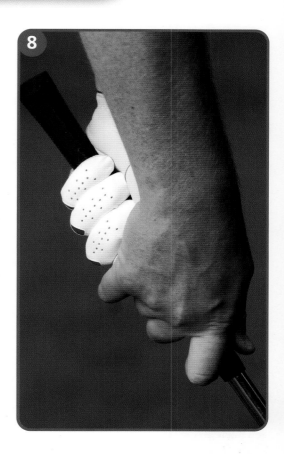

This is how *not* to grip it (7). You can see that I have no support on the club because I have gripped it too high. This is a common fault when a golfer is trying to hit the ball further.

I have gripped well down the shaft (8). This is great when hitting a short shot or even playing against the wind. This will increase the accuracy but will decrease the distance.

How not to grip it : Here are some common errors:

Too strong (9)

All the knuckles on the back of my left hand are on show, and both hands are gripping too far to the right of the golf club: this is what is known as a strong grip. This will cause the golf ball to hook (curve viciously right to left) because when you strike a golf ball your hands will want to rotate back into a neutral position, and this will cause the club face to close, resulting in a big right-to-left and very low flight.

Too weak (10)

My hands are positioned too far to the left of the golf club. Very few knuckles on the left hand are visible, and my right hand is too far to the left of the grip. Gripping the golf club this way will promote a high-flying slice/fade (curve left to right). The club face will open at impact, adding loft and creating the left-to-right spin.

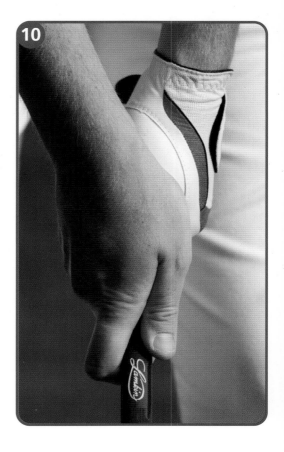

Build that stance *(For this sequence I am using a 6 iron)*

(1) I am now well into my set-up routine; I have aimed the club and I have gripped the club, so it's now time to build my stance.

To ensure that I maintain a consistent set-up position, I will strictly follow the step routine. I am going to take a step to the left approximately in line with my left shoulder (2).

I am then going to take an equal step to the right (3). I am now in position and almost ready to go. Notice how my stance is approximately shoulder-width apart and the ball position in the middle of my stance. The reason for having my feet shoulder-width apart is so I can make a good turn behind the ball; it is also worth noting that my weight is positioned evenly (50/50).

If I stand too wide or too narrow this will affect my shoulder turn and leg action; with the ball positioned in the middle of my stance, I can ensure that my club face is square to the target at impact. Poor ball position will affect the aim of my shoulders, consequently causing inconsistent golf shots.

Stand on those railway tracks – when building your stance you need to ensure that you position your feet, knees, hips and shoulders parallel to the ball-to-target-line. Think of it like standing on a railway track (4).

Here's how I get there:

Step 1

I am standing tall, my arms are stretched out in front of me, my legs are straight, my shoulders are back, my chin is up and the shaft of my golf club is completely horizontal. Notice how the club grip is pointing to my belt buckle.

(Step 1 inset) Note the face here and see how the very bottom of my golf club head is completely vertical.

Step 2

I have taken the squat position. My spine remains vertical and my golf club remains horizontal.

Step 3

I have now lowered my arms. The grip remains pointing to my belt buckle. Notice how my spine remains vertical. All I have done is just lowered my arms.

Step 4

Posture perfect. I have now tilted my body forward from the hips with my bottom pointing out. My body weight is perfectly balanced in the centre of my shoes and my arms are hanging naturally. Now I'm ready to go!

Posture – stand strong

I can have a perfect grip, I can align myself perfectly to the target; however I am not ready to start unless I have good posture. Posture holds the key when it comes to making consistent golf swings as you need to create a good spine angle. The best players maintain their spine angle throughout the golf swing.

(5) You can see that my knees are slightly flexed, my spine is straight, and I have tilted forward from my hips. My arms are hanging naturally and are approximately 6 inches away from my thighs. Notice how my chin is up: it's essential to get your chin up to allow you to make a full shoulder turn.

STEP 1

STEP 2

STEP 3

STEP 4

Golf Swing

The all important swing

Playing great golf requires consistency and repetition. The best players generally have the most simple golf swings – a simple turn behind the ball with the club on line at the top, then a simple turn through impact and hold a balanced through swing. If you have too many moving parts in your golf swing, you are going to struggle with your consistency.

Here are a few key thoughts and positions to help you on your way:

The takeaway (1a, 1b)

The one-piece move. Notice how my arms, shoulders and golf club have moved away as one. My head stays absolutely still. The golf club shaft at the half-way back stage is in line with my toes. The bottom edge of the club face is in line with my spine.

The set (2a, 2b)

When the golf club shaft moves beyond parallel with the ground, the weight of the club head causes the wrists to hinge a little. It's important to understand where the club shaft has to be at this point. The club is pointing just inside the line of the golf ball. This is what we call 'on plane'. If I wanted to go on and hit the ball from here without swinging the club any further, I would simply drop my arms and make good contact with the ball every time.

Golf Swing

At the top (3a, 3b)

My top half is fully wound up at this point. My shoulders have turned 90 degrees with my eyes remaining looking at the ball. Notice how my body weight has now moved to my back foot. The club position at the top is running parallel to my target line. The club face itself is in line with my left arm.

The top of the backswing is not what I call a static position: as soon as the club finds its way to the top, the body will start to unwind. I want you to understand that it is not a case of get to the top and then hit. Think: wind it up and then unwind!

Pull down (4a, 4b, 4c, 4d)

My body is turning to face the target and I am pulling the golf club into position. To start the downswing my hips are moving and rotating to face the target. I am pulling the golf club down with my left hand. Notice the golf club at the delivery position: the golf club is again in line with my shoes and ready to fire the golf ball towards the target. I see so many golfers hitting at the golf ball from the top (4b) or jumping up through impact (4d); both of these common faults will cause shots to go to the left and to the right and will also affect the strike of the ball.

Golf Swing

Impact

This doesn't look too dissimilar to my address position. At impact my hips are now turning to face the target and my body weight is now transferring to my left side. My right shoe is now rolling to the instep as I deliver the golf club to the back of the ball. My eyes remain focused on the ball. I try to watch the club head strike the ball.

Extend (6a, 6b, 6c)

To maximise your power and help improve your ball striking, extend your arms to the target. Think of it like keeping the club face looking at the target for as long as possible. This is the golfer's version of the knock-out punch. To really compress (squeeze) the golf ball, think about keeping the club face on the ball for as long as possible. Many golfers struggle to achieve this position, mainly because the direction of the downswing causes them to hit across the ball with a glancing blow. Try to achieve the extension position and it helps you hit it straighter and strike it better.

Golf Swing

Hold the pose (7a, 7b)

I believe that this is one of the most important positions. You may think that the golf ball is well on its way to the target so why is this so important? The golf swing doesn't stop when you strike the ball. The golf swing stops right at the very top. By achieving this position you are committing yourself to the golf shot. It will help you accelerate the golf club through impact and therefore will maximise your distance potential. It will also help with your ball striking. In achieving this follow-through position you will need great balance. Keeping your balance through impact will help you find the middle of the golf club more often. Notice how all the body weight is on my left side, my belt buckle is facing the target, the sole of my right shoe is pointing behind me and the club shaft is sitting on the back of my neck.

7a

7b

Driving

Driving

This is one of the most important parts of the game of golf. There is an old saying, 'Drive for show, putt for dough!' Great saying – however, driving is a lot more than just an act. If you have the ability to drive the golf ball a long way and also find the middle of the fairway every time, then the game becomes a lot easier. The world's greatest players are often great drivers.

The key to driving is sweeping the ball away and creating the optimum amount of spin. Too much spin sends the golf ball too high and too wide. Too little spin will not get the ball in the air.

How do I do it?

Key thought for driving:
'Swing the golf club' not **'Hit at the ball'**.

Good driving requires a strong, athletic address position (1)

I have adopted a wider stance with my driver. My feet are just a little wider than shoulder-width apart. This is because this golf club is longer than the others, therefore more club head speed will be generated. A wider base will help me keep good balance.

Notice how the golf ball is positioned just inside my left heel and my body weight would appear to be slightly favouring my right side. The reason for this is to help me sweep the golf ball away and prevent me hitting down on the ball, which will cause left and right shots and also the one that is popped up in the air.

Strong posture position (2)

My base is solid, my bottom is sticking out, and I've kept my chin up. This posture will allow me to make a nice full turn behind the ball. My arms are naturally hanging, I am not stretching for the ball, and neither am I too close and cramped. I am now alert and ready for the wind up.

Now wind it up (3, 4)

When winding up the power I have used the bigger muscles. My shoulders have turned 90 degrees, my knees have remained slightly flexed, and my eyes are still fully focused on the ball. It's important when making the backswing that you don't lose the width. Notice how the distance from my hands and chest at address has remained the same at the top of my backswing. Think: lower half firm, top half turn!

It's essential to stay in posture and not lift up to complete. I have turned around my spine angle, my left shoulder has turned under my chin, and my club shaft at the top is completely parallel to my toes and the target line.

It's time to unwind the power (5)

A common error I see in amateurs is that they try to hit at the golf ball with their arms and the top half of their body. As you can see, my lower half has initiated the downswing by rotating and moving to face the target. All I am thinking about is turning my hips to face the target and allowing the golf club to catch up!

Impact (6a, 6b)

My arms have now caught up, creating the snap. I am still in posture and still completely focused on the golf ball.

Driving

Pose for the cameras (7)

A key thought for the swing is to find your balance position. Although I have built up the power and released the golf club with tremendous speed, I have held a full follow-through position. What I mean by full is that the club head has now passed my right shoulder, my weight is now on my left foot, and the sole of my right shoe is pointing behind me. I am going to hold this position until the ball comes to rest. If I cannot hold my follow-through this is because I am off-balance, which will lead to missing hits and loss of power. Remember, it's not how hard you hit that sends the ball great distances, it's how well you hit. Stay in balance and find the middle of the club face more often.

How high do I tee it? Do what the pros do (8)!

Ideally, when hitting a driver I would like you to tee up the golf ball so that the ball is positioned towards the top half of the club face. This is ideal because if you want to drive it well you must sweep the ball away. I recommend that for the majority of your tee shots you tee the golf ball up in this position. A common fault that I see with tee height is when playing into the wind. People tend to tee the ball down, and this makes matters worse. If you tee it down you then have to strike down on the ball to make sure you get the ball airborne. When you strike down on the ball you then create too much spin which causes it to fly high. Remember, tee it to the top half of the club face and sweep.

If you have a hazard or trouble down the left of the fairway, I would like you to tee the golf ball down a fraction (9). When you tee the golf ball down, your angle of attack has to become slightly steeper. Due to the lack of loft on the driver the slight descending blow will promote back spin and slice/fade spin (left to right) taking your golf ball away from the trouble.

Where do I tee it up?

I see so many golfers just teeing the ball up in the centre of the teeing ground, with no real thought process. Course management is a vital part of the game. Be smart and play better.

Left is bad:

If you have trouble down the left side of a golf hole or you are fearful of hitting it to the left, then I want you to tee the golf ball up on the left side of the teeing ground (10). From the left side I am now looking away from the danger. It opens up the golf hole and will assist with me hitting my drive away from the trouble down the left side. Notice how I am standing outside the teeing ground. As long as the ball remains inside the teeing area you are fine. Some people feel that the marker is a distraction; if this sounds like you, position your feet inside the tee marker. Having the tee marker between me and the ball isn't a problem for me. I know to hit the tee marker it would have to be a very bad swing…

Right is bad:

If you have trouble down the right side of the hole or if your bad shot always goes to the right, then I want you to tee the golf ball up on the right side of the teeing ground (11). By teeing the golf ball up on the right side, again you are looking away from the trouble; this will assist with hitting your drive away from the trouble down the right side.

Try these very simple but very effective tips and you're sure to improve your golf game.

Long Irons

The long irons are generally made up of 1, 2, 3, 4 and 5 irons; they are, however, being used less and less, with the modern day golfer opting for a hybrid golf club or a high lofted fairway metal. Having said that, the long iron is still a favourite for the tournament professional and is used by many golfers playing their golf on the seaside courses where keeping it low is imperative.

Why is the long iron so difficult to use?

The long iron will flight the ball with a low trajectory; this is mainly due to the little loft and the shape of the head. The head is very slim and with little mass at the back of the golf club this results in low flighted shots. Some of the manufacturers now design their long irons with a big thick sole and weight behind the club face; this will help flight the ball higher.

The sweet spot is harder to find because the club is now longer. It's often said to be a true test for a golfer to be able to strike a long iron shot.

Practice the harder shots

I often hear golfers complaining that they can't hit with their long irons and I also hear of many golfers leaving their long irons in the garage, or in the car; this can restrict them to only 12 or 13 clubs.

To be a good long game player you need to be a good striker of the ball. It is a test for the amateur golfer to hit a long iron. I don't see enough players practising with their long irons. When I go to the driving range I often see people smashing drivers as hard as they can and hitting their trusty 7 iron for warm up, but you very rarely see them practising with the long iron. The reason is that they probably struggle to hit with it and they don't want to be seen hitting poor shots on the driving range.

How do I hit my long irons?

It's all in the set up. I always say the golf swing is the same with every club in the bag, the length of the club will change the swing plane, the set up will change the way you strike the ball. Hitting a good long iron requires a shallow angle of attack so the ball can be swept away without taking too much divot. How? It's in the set up:

As with every shot, start off with your feet and knees together and the ball positioned in the centre of the stance (1).

Take a small step to the left and then a bigger step to the right (2).

Your feet should ideally be just a little wider than your shoulders. Notice how my spine is tilted slightly to the right, my head is positioned slightly behind the ball, my hands are positioned opposite the ball and my feet are slightly further apart. With all these factors taken into consideration it will encourage a wider swing arc and will encourage a sweeping motion through the all-important hitting area (3).

It's essential to strike the ball well when hitting the long iron. You will notice that the ball is slightly further up in the stance; it's easy when moving the ball forward to hit the ground before the ball. I want you to focus on one of the dimples on top of the ball.

A great thought to have in the swing is: "wide and rhythm". This is so simple but very effective. Wide means wide away and wide through, rhythm means not hurried. Golfers get anxious and try to force the issue; think rhythm and sweep it away time after time, not forgetting to hold a full balanced follow-through (4, 5, 6).

Fairway Metals

The fairway metal is still the golfer's favourite. You will still hear them referred to as fairway woods, this is because the old wooden head was so popular for many years. The terminology remains the same – old habits die hard.

Many golfers still opt for the fairway metal from the tee because they're not overly confident with the driver. The added loft and shorter shaft length will help keep it straighter and find more fairways.

Being able to hit the fairway woods will help you reach the longer par 4's and par 5 holes in 2 shots, creating good par and birdie opportunities.

The fairway metal is a favourite for the lady golfer, the senior golfer and the general mid- to high-handicapper. This is due to the difficulty in striking with the long iron, therefore the fairway metal is a great alternative.

The loft of a fairway metal is typically 15 degrees for a standard 3-metal, 19 degrees for a 5-metal, and 24 degrees for a 7-metal.

The 5-metal loft is comparable to the 2 iron; the 7-metal is comparable to a 4-iron.

Why are fairway metals so popular?

- It has a larger club head. When compared to the iron this gives you greater stability, due the fact that it is less likely to twist at impact, giving the golfer a straighter ball flight.
- The weight is concentrated to the sole of the club creating a lower centre of gravity to help get the ball airborne. The sweet spot is also larger than that of the long iron.
- The shape of the sole allows the club to sweep the ball away rather than digging into the turf.
- The club is longer than the long iron, giving you more club head speed.

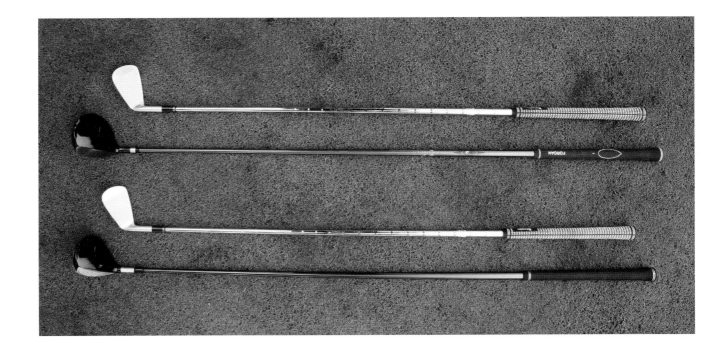

How to nail your fairway metals (1, 2, 3)

The set-up holds the key when hitting the fairway metals. I want you to sweep the ball away and not dig at it, in a similar way as in driving.

Ball Position

To assist with the sweep I want you to position the golf ball forward in your stance: not quite in line with your left heel but mid-way between your left heel and the centre of the stance.

Body weight

Position your body weight evenly; however, it should feel as though your left shoulder is slightly higher and that you are tilted slightly behind the ball.

Stance

A good solid base is needed when playing the fairway metals. This is to obtain solid balance throughout the golf swing and encourage a wider swing arc to promote the sweep.

Step to it to find the perfect position

Start off by having your feet and knees together and the ball positioned in the centre of your shoes. Take a small step to the left, approximately 5 inches, then take a bigger step to the right. You should find that the ball is half way between the centre and your left heel. Be careful not to stand at driver width for the fairway metals, as this will restrict your body turn and will create a loss of power.

Sweep it away (4, 5, 6, 7, 8 - next page)

A great thought for when hitting the fairway woods: 'Complete the golf swing and let the ball get in the way of the travelling club head'. This will stop you from hitting at the ball and will promote a nice flowing golf swing that sweeps it off the fairway time and time again.

Hybrids

The Hybrid/Rescue club has revolutionised the game of golf today; it an extremely useful tool which is now every golfer's 'must-have' accessory. It is a very forgiving club that is designed to send the golf ball up in the air with a high trajectory. It can be used out of the rough, it can be used from a poor lie, it can be used off the tee, it can be used from the fairway and it can also be used to chip with.

It is not quite a wood and not quite an iron but somewhere in between. It is the length of a long iron but has similar characteristics to a fairway wood.

How can a golf club do all that?

The term 'Hybrid' means mixed origin or composition. In the golf world it means that the components of wood and irons have been mixed together to produce the ever-popular hybrid.

The shorter length in the shaft will help you control the club head, thereby increasing consistency and centre strikes. The fairway metal is long, whereas the hybrid club is similar in length to the long iron. The wide sole of the golf club and lower centre of gravity combine to create a large sweet spot and will send the golf ball skywards very quickly.

It has a shallow face to ensure that every time you strike the ball from a tight lie you will always find the centre of the club face and not the bottom, which is often the case with the fairway woods.

The set-up when playing the hybrid club is very similar to the long irons. Always use the step, step method to be sure of perfect ball position (2, 3, 4).

Notice how I have started with my feet and knees absolutely together and the ball positioned in the centre of my shoes. I have taken a small step and a bigger step to the right so that the ball is slightly forward of centre. My feet are just a fraction wider than my shoulders (as with the long iron). The body weight should remain 50/50.

With the forward ball position and the slightly wider stance, again, this will promote a sweeping action. Think sweep, not dig, when playing the hybrids.

Hybrids

Chip with the Hybrid (5, 6, 7, 8)

The hybrid can often be a smart club to use when you are just off the putting surfaces. If you have a poor lie, or you are afraid of fluffing the shot (hitting the ground before the ball), then this is a smart shot to play.

Play the shot just like a chip and run shot. Set up with your body weight favouring your left side, opt for the putter grip and think 'putt with the hybrid'. The large sole will prevent the club from digging into the turf, the slight loft of the club will loft the ball for a short period and then it will let it roll to the target.

Spend some time practising this method before using it in competition. It will be different from your usual chipping clubs. The hybrid club has less loft for a start, so the ball will roll further. The strike will be different from one with the iron, it will be more powerful, so a shorter, softer swing is needed here for this shot.

Hybrid out of a bad lie (9, 10, 11, 12)

When you have a long way to reach the green and you find your ball in a bad lie, such as a divot or the rough, the hybrid can be a good option. Playing this shot with an iron can nearly be impossible, because the club head digs into the long grass turning the club head over and causing the golf ball to fly to the left of the target. The shape of the hybrid will prevent the club from digging in and result in straighter, longer shots.

To play the hybrid out of a bad lie does require a descending blow to the golf ball. Move back from the ball a fraction in your stance and feel as if you're hitting down on the ball. The usual sweeping motion will not work from a bad lie.

I'm not saying that you should always use a hybrid from a bad lie. However it is a good option if you have a long way to go to reach the target and you don't feel too confident with a fairway wood or a long iron.

Mid Irons

What are the mid irons?

The mid irons are the 6, 7 and 8 irons. They are your approach clubs, the flag finders. It's important that you understand some key facts about the mid irons. If you can master these clubs you would certainly reduce your handicap.

The perfect starting club

If you are new to the game these are the clubs that I would recommend you to practise with. The reason for this is simple; they are not too long, they are not too short, they have a reasonable amount of loft, without having too much loft. They are the in-between club, and make the perfect practice club. Beginner or professional, when working on your golf swing, I would recommend that you use a mid iron – it's the obvious choice when practising.

The correct way to strike it!

Here are a few tips to help you understand the correct way to strike the ball. Many people think that you should strike an iron without taking a divot. Many people really aren't too sure what happens so a little explanation is needed. Imagine striking the ball with a descending blow, keeping in mind the idea: ball followed by a slight divot. However, the last thing you should do is go out there and smash down on the ball. Remember, it's all in the set-up and the correct transition.

The 3 different ball positions

As you can see in the pictures you basically have 3 different ball positions in golf, for the 3 different shots.

The Driver ball position is forward in the stance to promote the sweep (3).

The Mid iron ball position is in the centre of the stance to promote the crisp ball – divot strike (4).

The Wedge ball position is back in the stance to promote the descending blow (5).

The Set-up

When playing the mid irons, your body weight should be distributed absolutely 50/50. Your feet should be shoulder-width apart and your weight should be evenly spread between your heels and your toes. When standing to the ball let your arms hang freely. Ideally, the grip of the golf club should be approximately a hand's width from the inside of your left thigh.

The Swing (6, 7)

When hitting the irons I want you to swing the club within yourself. Don't take it back too far. Notice here at the top of the backswing, the golf club hasn't made it to the parallel position. It's not quite three-quarters and not quite parallel. It's controlled. My shoulders, however, have turned 90 degrees and my back is facing the target.

The speed of the swing is important to become a good mid iron player. Swing the golf club with good rhythm and keep a good balance. Remember, it's not how hard you hit it that will send it close to the target, it's how well prepared you are and how well you hit it! You have much more chance of finding the middle of the club face if you swing the club within yourself whilst keeping good balance.

Always try to hold a balanced follow-through, until the ball has landed. Notice how the golf club is resting just in the base of my neck. Finding this position will help accelerate the golf club through the all-important hitting area.

Short Irons

Short Irons

The short irons are the 9-iron, Pitching Wedge, Gap Wedge, Sand Wedge and Lob Wedge (1). They are known as the scoring clubs. These clubs are generally used from 125 yards and closer. You can have a poor long game, but if this part of your game is in good shape then you'll be hard to beat.

This is the part of the game that separates the pros from the amateurs, the world-beater from the journeyman professional.

Home in on the pin with those short shots

Here are a few pointers to help you home in:

Alignment is very important with the short shots. Take extra care making sure that your club face is pointing towards your target. Step back, pick your target line, align the club face first of all, and then take your grip and position your body (2). It's a cardinal sin to miss the green with a short iron.

Ball back, weight forward and narrow stance

Move the ball slightly further back in the stance: halfway between centre and your back foot is ideal (3). This will ensure that you make contact with the ball before the turf.

A common error for many golfers is that they try to lift the ball up in the air. This causes all sorts of striking and direction problems. You should strike down on the ball.

Position your body weight towards your left side, approximately 55/45, favouring your left side. This will promote a steeper swing angle, in turn promoting a downward blow to the ball (4).

Stand a fraction narrower. This will encourage a shorter controlled swing. The wider you stand the bigger and more powerful your swing will become. With the scoring clubs, you don't want power, you need precision.

Swing Thought: Think – slightly shorter swing and keep compact

When hitting the short irons I want your back swing to mirror the through-swing in length, three-quarter length back and three-quarter length through shots (5, 6). Do not over-swing when playing the shorter shots.

Know your distances

It's important to know how far you hit every club in your bag, but it's essential that you know how far you hit your short irons. Depending on how much golf you play you should always keep a check of your distances. The more often you play, the more often you need to check.

> **How do I find out how far?**
>
> *Find a flat piece of ground, maybe the practice area at your club. Make sure it's a still day as wind will affect the results.*
>
> *Use the same golf balls that you would normally use in competition. Do not use range balls because they do not fly in the same way as the normal golf ball.*
>
> *Make steady swings and think '90 degrees'. Swing within yourself to hit it closer. The harder you hit it, the wider you will hit it.*
>
> *Hit 10 counting shots with each of your short irons. Don't count the missed hits, play another ball.*
>
> *Pace out the yardage (or use markers) of every single shot that you hit that counted.*
>
> *To calculate the average, add up the total yardage of all the balls that counted, and divide the total by the total number of shots taken that counted.*
>
> *It makes the game so much easier when you know how far you hit the golf ball with your short irons. If you are faced with a challenging short-iron shot and know the yardage, all you have to do is pick the correct club and trust the swing.*

Pitching

What is a pitch?

A pitch is a shot usually played from within 100 yards of the target, using a pitching wedge, sand wedge or a lob wedge. The golf ball will spend the majority of its journey in the air. Pitching is often referred to as the 'scoring game'. Lots of golfers can hit the ball great distances and have the most beautiful golf swings, but the golfers who pitch it well, generally will score very well. Pitching is often the pro's favourite but not a favourite for the amateur golfer. It's an in-between shot, not too short and not too long. It's all about controlling the distance.

How do I pitch it?

I want you to understand the correct way to strike the golf ball when pitching. Strike the ball with a slight descending blow – ball first is a must.

Many golfers misunderstand the concept of pitching. A common fault is when the golfer tries to help the ball in the air, with excessive wrist action.

Grip: The grip remains very similar to when hitting a full shot. However my grip pressure is slightly lighter; this will help promote extra feel and gain control of distance. Notice how I have also gripped lower down the handle; this will help give me more control and take the power out of the shot. The tighter and higher you grip the more power will be generated.

The last thing you want when pitching is power.

Grip it low for feel: I have a very simple set-up procedure for this.

If I am faced with a standard length pitch then I will grip it 3 fingers down the handle (1). I should be able to fit 3 fingers on my right from my little finger to the top of the grip.

If I have a very short pitch then I will grip 4 fingers down the handle (2). If I'm faced with a longer pitch/full swing then I will grip the club at its full length with 2 fingers.

Weaken to land drop and stop:

When gripping the golf club turn your hands a fraction to the left of the grip (3). When glancing down (without moving your head) one to one-and-a-half knuckles should be visible on the back of your left hand. This will cause the club face to open a fraction at impact, preventing the club digging in and of course giving you extra height with a soft landing.

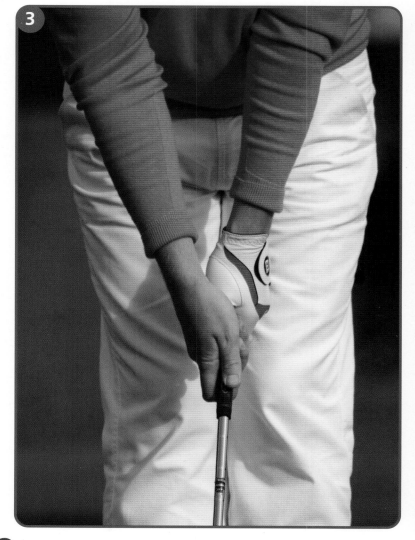

Stance (4):

Notice that I have opted for a narrow stance for this pitch shot. The shorter the shot, the shorter the swing. By standing narrower you are forced to make a short swing. If you attempt to make a longer swing you will lose your balance.

Ball position: Look how the golf ball is positioned opposite my chin. (Please note it's not directly under my chin but opposite.) This is the lowest point of the arc of the swing. It is also the point when my club will bottom out. You'll also notice that the ball is positioned slightly towards the back half of my stance; again this will help promote a crisp strike.

Body weight: My body weight is positioned towards my left side 60/40. This will promote a slightly steeper golf swing and steeper angle of attack, striking down on the ball, which is the perfect way to strike it.

Hand position: My hands are slightly ahead of the ball. This again will help with ball striking.

4

Pitching posture (5):

You can now see that due to gripping further down the handle, I am standing quite close to the ball. You can see how I'm bending forward from my hips. My arms are hanging naturally. I am in a comfortable balanced position and ready to hit it close. Top tip – 'let your arms hang, don't stretch'.

Alignment – open up: From this position you can see some interesting facts about pitching. Notice how my shoulders are running completely parallel to the target. However my feet are pointing to the left of the target, I have withdrawn my left foot and moved my left hip slightly back out of the way. This is to help me swing the club slightly steeper (more upright) and more importantly it allows me to hold the club face square through impact. If my left hip was square I would then run the risk of hitting myself in the left thigh.

Pitching

It's all in the set-up!

Your set-up position is also your impact position.

For this sequence I'm playing a 50-yard pitch shot with my 54-degree wedge (strong sand wedge).

The pitching swing (6)

To be a good pitcher of the golf ball you need to be able to control your distance. To help you achieve great distance control I want you to try and get your arms, body and golf club working together without excessive wrist action. Too much wrist action gives you unwanted and uncontrollable power. Notice when I move the golf club away from the ball I have retained the "Y" shape: my shoulders, arms and golf club have worked together. My body weight started on the left side and it has stayed on the left side. There is no sign of weight transference when pitching. Transferring my body weight would give me unwanted power and could also cause inconsistent strikes.

(7) The golf club is in front of my body. In other words the club has not moved around my body. If you compare this backswing position to the backswing position in the golf swing section you will notice the golf club shaft is now pointing slightly to the left of the target. This is due to the weight position and also the withdrawal of my left shoe.

At impact (8)

My impact position is very similar to my set-up position. You can see how my body weight is still slightly favouring my left side, and notice how my hands remain ahead of the ball.

The follow-through (9)

Again I have retained the 'Y' shape. Arms, body and golf club have worked together. My body weight has remained on my left side and my chest is facing the target. As you can see, my wrists have remained passive throughout the swing.

Pitching swing thought

You can see in the sequence of pictures that the back swing and through swing are very similar in length. Think 'same distance back, same distance through'.

I know that you can't see this in actual speed but I can assure you that the speed of the swing is also constant. 'Same speed back, same speed through'.

TOP TIP:
'same distance back, same distance through' and 'same speed back, same speed through'.

Finding your distances (10, 11, 12)

It's important that you know how far you hit the ball. Measure your full shot distances with all of your wedges. When measuring it's important you don't try to force it: think 90 per cent. If you can measure your full shot distances, your three-quarter swing distances and also your half-swing distances, you'll have a good idea of how far you actually hit the ball. You will see a great improvement with your pitching.

The longer the shot, the wider you stand, the higher you grip and the longer you swing it. Notice that here I'm faced with a 75-yard shot. My back swing has increased and so has the through-swing; the speed, however, has remained constant.

Common Errors

Poor ball position:

I see so many golfers playing the ball too far back in their stance (13). When the ball is positioned too far back it de-lofts the golf club. Golfers are often well aware that the ball is too far back, and you'll find them reverting back to their right side (14) at impact to make contact with the golf ball, resulting in heavy shots (ground first) or thin shots (striking the ball halfway up).

Too far forward will cause heavy shots (ground first) and can also send the ball too high and short of distance due to the added loft. This is often known as the 'the scoop' (15) and is a common error, especially if there is a hazard between you and the hole. The golfer will try and help the ball up in the air. This causes all sorts of problems: heavy shots (hitting the ground first), thin shots (hitting the ball halfway up), flop shots (too high, nowhere near). All of these shots are common to the club golfer and can ruin the score card.

Too narrow and too much wrist (16)

My arms have collapsed and my wrists are fully hinged, resulting in too much club head speed, making it impossible to judge the strike and distance. For me to make contact with the ball, I need to straighten my arms and also unhinge my wrist.

Lean back (17)

This is one of the biggest faults of all. This will cause heavy shots and thin shots, and also make it impossible to judge distance control.

Chipping

What is a chip shot?

It is a shot played from close to the putting surface. Think of it like a long putt with the iron. The golf ball will spend a short time in the air but will spend the majority of its journey on the ground. It is a shot played with all of the irons, not just your favourite wedge. Some pros nowadays actually chip the golf ball with their fairway metals or hybrids. Often a golfer will have their favourite club for playing the chip shot. When playing the chip shot try to land the ball on the green as soon as possible, which means that you will sometimes be required to use a straighter faced club. When using a straighter faced club the swing will be shorter, the strike will be better therefore gaining consistency.

I do my A-B-C every time I am faced with a chip shot. Your ball is sitting at point A, and to get to point C you need to find a point B. Pick out your point B approximately two paces on the green. Once you've read this I'm sure that you will want to get out there and start practising your own A-B-C of chipping.

Set Up

Think of a chip shot as a shorter version of the pitch shot. As with the pitch shot the set up is absolutely crucial. I want you to maintain your set-up position throughout the swing. This means absolutely no weight transference. Transferring the body weight from the right to the left will only encourage missed hits and poor distance control. The closer you are to the target the smaller you are going to make yourself. This means you must grip the club lower, keep a narrower stance, and stand closer.

Aim

Just like the full swing it's crucial that you aim the club face to where you intend the golf ball to go. Remember this does not necessarily mean you should always aim at the target; more often than not you will have some slopes to deal with. I want you to try and land the ball on the green as quickly as possible and let it run towards the hole. I try to look for a point approximately two paces on to the green (1).

I have marked the point where I want to land the ball with a tee peg (please note that this is only for practice: you cannot place an object on the green in competition). As soon as I have picked my point to land the ball (point B), I then need to ask myself the question 'What club is it going to take to land the ball at this spot and then run out to the target?' This is where lots of golfers lose so many shots. They are so concerned about how to get it close to the hole, that they forget where to land the ball, leading to lack of direction and poor distance control. When you are sure that you have got the correct club for the task ahead, take great care in aiming the club face to the landing point. Stand behind the ball and pick out your target line. When you are happy with your aim, position your feet and knees absolutely together, with the golf ball in the centre of your stance (2, 3).

Chipping

Grip

There are different ways of gripping the golf club when chipping the golf ball. However the one key thought always remains constant: 'grip it light'. This will help promote extra feeling for the shot and help you obtain greater distance control.

I generally will advise two different grips for chipping: the putting grip (4) and the normal grip (5).

Notice that with the normal grip I have slightly weakened my left hand. The back of my left hand is now facing the target.

I tend to use the putting grip for the shorter chip shots. The putting grip will help to reduce the wrist action and keep the club face square to the target throughout the swing. The normal grip can often encourage a little wrist action and will also assist with rotation of the club, ideal for the longer shots. Again, similar to pitching, I want you to vary the position of your hands for the different lengths of shot.

I have got a short shot so I have gone four fingers down the handle (6). The shorter the shot, the lower you grip it. This is because when you grip down the handle you make the club shorter, therefore taking the power out of the shot. The longer the shot, the higher you should grip it, and the longer the club, the longer the levers, thus giving you more power.

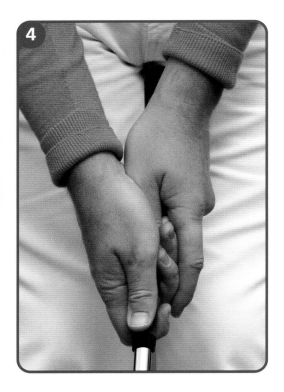

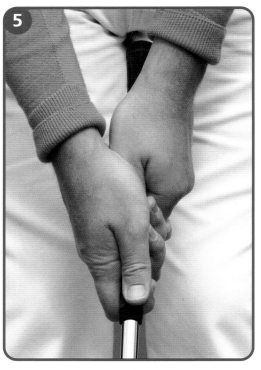

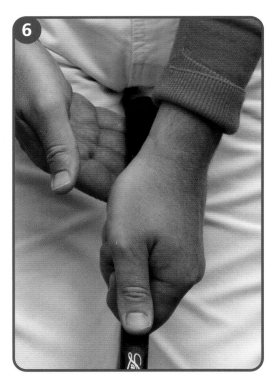

Stance and ball position (7)

Notice how I have slightly widened my stance for the shot ahead. My stance however is still narrow. The golf ball is directly opposite my chin and my hands are slightly ahead of the ball. Remember the longer the shot, the wider you stand, the shorter the shot, the narrower you should stand.

My shoulder line is running parallel to the target, however, my feet are pointing to the left of the target (open). Due to the length of the shot I am now gripping lower and would appear to be standing closer to the ball. (8) I have withdrawn my left shoe and hip to give me more room when making contact with the ball, and this will help me hold the club face square for longer.

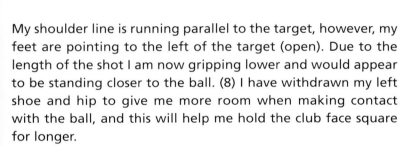

Body weight (9)

My body weight is favouring my left side. This will encourage me to strike down on the ball with a slight descending blow allowing the golf ball to climb the grooves on the club and make its way in the air. My weight will remain on this side when making the golf swing. Think: pivot around your left side. Weight transference gives poor chip shots.

Chipping

Find the swing (10, 11, 12, 13, 14, 15)

When you are happy with your landing point and you are happy with your club selection, I want you to make some rehearsal swings. When making these swings I want you to try and 'find the swing' that will land your golf ball on your secondary target in position to complete the hole. This may take two, three or even four practice swings. Once you are happy with the length and speed then go and repeat that exact swing on the golf ball.

Shoulders, arms and golf club are moving together. Think of the chipping swing as like a long putt. Notice that there is very little wrist action for this shot. My body weight has remained on my left side; my shoulders are slightly rotating and controlling the club head.

Notice how the golf club has moved back and through the same distance. Always hold the pose. The club face remains pointing at the target all the while as the ball comes to the end of its journey.

Chipping

Common errors

Poor ball and weight position (16, 17, 18)

You can see the ball is positioned too far forward with body weight back on the right side; this will encourage the golfer to strike the ball on the upswing, risking the thin shot (hit halfway up the ball); it also adds more loft to the golf club so that the ball often rises too high and finishes short of the target. It will also promote a very wristy action, which will lead to poor distance control.

Ball back (19, 20, 21)

Having the ball close to the feet, and the hands so far forward, takes away the loft from the golf club. The back swing becomes very steep. During the swing the golfer's body will often fall back to the right side at impact as he tries to loft the ball in the air, resulting in poor strikes and distance control.

Poor swing path

Here you can see two completely different back swings. The golf club should travel back in a reasonably straight line. You can see that when correctly using my arms and shoulders, the club head remains in front of my body (22). A common error I see is when the back swing is too flat (rounded). The golf club goes behind the body, which encourages excessive use of the wrists and hands to attempt to keep the ball on track (23). The likely outcome when the club moves this way is a thin shot (ball struck halfway up) with poor direction control, caused by the rounded swing path, and also poor distance control caused by the excessive use of the wrists and closing of the club face.

Poor club selection

One of the most common errors I see with chipping is poor club selection and decision making. Hopefully, once you have read this you will have a better idea of how to play the chip shots. Just think A-B-C.

Putting

Putting is without any question the most important part of the game. After all, the objective of the game of golf is to get that little ball into the hole in the fewest number of shots. So many golfers will spend lots of time perfecting their golf swings and trying to hit the ball great distances, but generally not enough time is spent on the short game, putting in particular.

All the great champions past and present have got this uncanny ability to get the ball in the hole when it really matters. Tiger Woods is often thought of as being one of the longest hitters on tour and having a golf swing to die for. However, Tiger Woods just happens to be one of the best putters in the world.

Why all the funny shapes? (1)

These are just a small selection of putters designed by Scotty Cameron. He is well known across the globe for his putter designs. His putters are used by professional golfers around the world. He designs the putters for Titleist, who are currently a leading brand in the market place.

Choice of putter is very much a personal thing. If you like the look and feel of a putter, then the chances are you are going to use it quite well. The putter must be the correct length for you. The standard length of a man's putter is 35 inches long. This is fine if you are Mr Average, but everyone is different. Your height should not actually determine your putter length because you may have short or long arms. I am 6ft 1inch and my putter is 34 inches long, which is actually 1 inch shorter than standard. This is because I have long arms. Notice with these putters that the heads are different shapes, and the way the shaft enters the putter head is also different in each case. The reason for the different design is to help you as an individual to find a putter that best suits your putting stroke.

Perfect your putting (2, 3, 4, 5)

Now I want you to understand the importance of the putting stroke; see how I build a stroke that will definitely work.

Notice how I have slightly bent forward from the hips and I have placed my hands together. My arms are hanging naturally and my feet are approximately shoulder-width apart. I want you to now imagine that you are a 'grandfather clock'. The whole of your body is going to remain absolutely still, your hands, arms and shoulders are going to act as the 'pendulum'.

Notice how my hands, arms and shoulders are working together and creating a rocking motion. This is the perfect way to putt because you are using the bigger muscles therefore the stroke will be able to repeat itself. When you put this into practice, try to keep the whole of your body still, just let your arms and shoulders work together. Don't let your body swing the putter, don't let your wrist swing the putter, keep the triangle together. You will feel that you are pivoting from your fulcrum point, which is at the very base of your neck. The hands are moving in a straight line back and through.

Putting

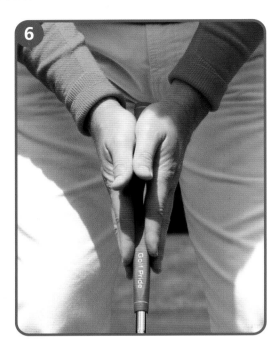

Time to take the grip

There are many different ways to grip the putter. I want to grip the putter in such a way that I can control the stroke, but I also want to grip the putter in such a way that my hands are passive. I do not want excessive use of my hands when putting; I also do not want to rotate the putter face.

It would be perfect if I could grip the putter with my hands together; however, this would not be ideal because it would be impossible for me to control the putter during the stroke.

You will notice that the putter grip itself is different to a normal grip. A normal grip is circular, but the putter grip is flat at the top. Providing the manufacturer has done a good job and fitted the grip squarely, then the flat part of the grip should be completely square to the putter face (6).

When I place my hands on the putter grip I am going to do it in such a way that my palms are facing each other. My right hand is now below my left, just as when hitting the full shot (7).

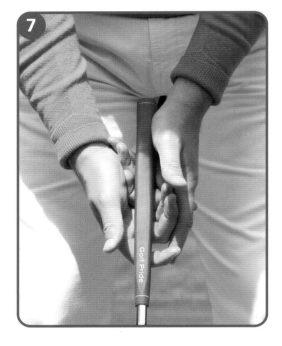

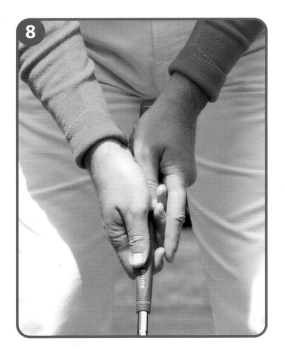

I have now gripped the putter, and the index finger on my left hand is overlapping my fingers of my right hand. This grip is known as "the reverse overlap" (8). This is the common putter grip used by many professional golfers, including Tiger Woods. Gripping the putter this way will prevent me from rotating the putter during the stroke, and it will keep the wrist action to a minimum. My thumbs form a straight line down the top of the putter grip. They are sitting on the flat part of the grip. With my thumbs in a straight line, my hands should be square to the putter face.

The different grips

Left Below Right (9)

This is also a common way of gripping the putter. The palms again are facing each other, the thumbs are in a straight line, but the hands have changed round. The left below right grip is good if you have a tendency of hitting at the ball, or flicking when putting. The left hand acts as guide hand through the stroke, making it impossible to hit at the ball with the right hand.

The Claw (10)

This grip is a relatively new one to the game. It was made famous by Chris DiMarco (US Tour Professional and Ryder Cup Player). The left hand secures the putter and the right hand guides the putter throughout the stroke. It is now a very common grip used by many golfers.

There are many other ways to grip the putter, but I chose these three because I feel that they are the best way to give you a consistent stroke that will hole putts.

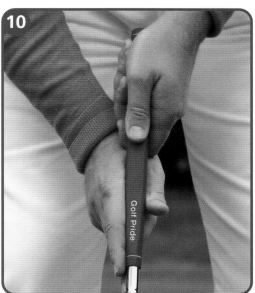

Build the stance

Just as with the golf swing I am going to begin by positioning my feet and knees absolutely together. The golf ball is positioned in the centre of my stance (11). When I am happy with the aim of the putter face, I am then going to take a small step to the left (12) and then a slightly bigger step to the right (13). You will notice that the ball is positioned slightly forward in my stance. This will help promote a slight upward strike on the golf ball improving the roll. My stance is approximately shoulder-width apart. I like to stand with my feet shoulder-width apart because it helps me stay still and in balance throughout the stroke.

Putting

Eyes over (14, 15, 16, 17)

This is a great tip for good putting – when you address the golf ball, I want you to hold your body position, close your left eye, put a ball over your closed eye, drop it and see where it lands. Ideally it should land directly on top of the object ball. This is shown in this sequence. It's essential to get your eyes over the ball because it helps with the aiming of the putter.

Stand square (18)

To illustrate the Stand Square I have placed two wooden blocks on the green, forming a perfectly straight corridor towards the hole. My feet, knees, hips and most importantly my shoulders are completely parallel to my intended target. From this square position I can rock my shoulders like a pendulum and I can be sure that my putter is going to move back and through in a perfectly straight line.

Stroke it (19, 20)

Having mentioned the 'grandfather clock' earlier, now it's time to put it to the test. Providing your set up and alignment is good, there should be no reason to miss a putt. This is only of course if you are able to judge the correct distance. When making the putting stroke I want the putter to go back and through, the exact same distance and speed. Think:

'Same distance back, same distance through – Same speed back, same speed through'. Remember, stay still and keep the stroke constant.

The length and speed of the stroke will change depending on the length of the putt. The longer the putt, the longer the stroke, the shorter the putt the shorter the stroke – simple! I see so many golfers varying the length and speed of the stroke; this causes missed putts and poor distance control. Don't look too soon. I try and keep my head still until my putter has completed the stroke. Once I have completed the through-swing that's when I will have a look to see if it's going in.

Paint the line (21, 22, 23)

Another great thought to have when putting is to paint the straight line. Imagine that your putter head is a paint brush. I want you to paint a complete straight line when making the stroke. If the line is like a zigzag then you are likely to miss the putt. A great way to practice a perfect stoke is to hit putt after putt from between the two blocks. This is great because when you address the ball you can see if you're standing square to the ball. You can also groove the perfect stroke by avoiding the blocks when hitting the putts. I would advise that you try to hole 50 putts from 5ft with the blocks on the green. See how you get on; with a bit of practice you shouldn't miss any. Once you have completed 50 putts, try 100. If you don't have any blocks, you can always lay two of your clubs on the green, with the grips pointing towards the hole (3- & 4- iron).

Putting

Reading the green

Reading the green is essential to becoming a good putter. Here are a few tips to help you become a great putter.

The main read (24)

This is directly behind the ball and in line with the intended target. What I am looking for here are the noticeable slopes on the green between my ball and the hole. I examine the terrain surrounding the green and carefully study the slopes that will affect the direction of my golf ball. Ask yourself the question: If it pours down with rain where would the water go? Where would the puddles be? I also try and break up the path of the putt into three stages, and try to figure out which way the putt is going to move through those three different stages.

From behind (25)

If there was any doubt with the main read then this is where your mind is made up. From behind the hole you can get a completely different perspective on which way the ball will go. You have a better view of what will happen at the all-important end of the journey.

Up or down? (26)

Many golfers ignore this view, which is a big mistake. You can clearly see from here the way the slope will affect the speed of the putt. Is it uphill or is it downhill, or is it both up and down?

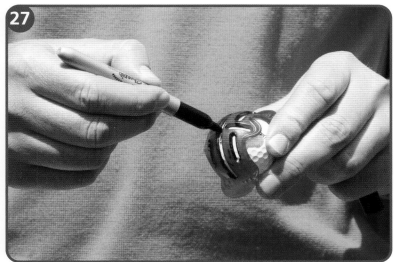

Line it up

This is an essential tool that I would never be without. It's a simple plastic template I use to mark a bold black line on my golf ball. I use the black line to line up my putts. Many tour professionals use the line method to help with their alignment for putting (27, 28).

When I am happy with my read, I will very carefully replace my golf ball and line up the black line on the ball towards my intended target (29). This doesn't necessarily have to be the hole.

I have placed a tee peg in the ground just outside the hole. I have placed it there because this is the point I need to aim at to hole the putt. I have replaced my golf ball, with the line pointing towards my intended target (tee peg). When addressing the golf ball I will line up the line on my golf ball with the line on my putter (30).

Once I strike the putt I will gain feedback from how the golf ball rolls. If the golf ball rolls end over end and the black line doesn't deviate then I know that I have hit a good putt. If it rolls end over end and I happen to miss the putt then I know that I have hit a good putt but I will need to question my read of the terrain. If, however, the line deviates, then I can question my stroke, because I obviously haven't hit the putt that I intended to.

Putting

Putting practice games & drills

As I have already mentioned, putting is probably the most important part of the game. It is also the part of the game that most golfers practise the least. Why? Well, I often hear golfers complaining that putting practice is boring. I would agree that it's not too much fun standing on a green trying to hole putts aimlessly. That is why I have set up a few games and drills to help bring the fun back to your putting practice and ultimately improve your putting. Like everything in life, you need goals to improve. Try some of the following and see how you get on:

Around the clock (31, 32, 33)

This is a great game to really improve your putting. I have carefully placed 12 golf balls around a hole. They are equally positioned around the hole and I have measured them at a 5-iron distance from the hole (3 feet). The objective here is to hole as many putts as I can around the clock. Each and every putt will be different. They are all the same length but the green is slightly sloping, which means that every putt will have a different borrow to it. Take your time and work your way around the clock. You have only mastered this exercise when you can achieve 12 out of 12, six times in a row.

Ladder putting (34, 35, 36, 37, 38)

Again using 12 golf balls, I have set up my very own golfing ladder, as you can see, and as the putt gets longer the balls are getting slightly further apart. Similar to the clock, with the ladder I want you to test yourself and see how many putts you can hole. This time the line of the putt will be constant throughout but your pace will be tested here. You will feel the stroke increase as you climb the ladder. Remember, try to keep the putting stroke at a constant speed and also match the length of the backswing with the through-swing. Watch closely when you hit the shorter putts as this will give you feedback for the remaining putts, since they will be taking exactly the same line. The ladder is harder than the clock. I want you to hole all 12 putts three times in a row.

Distance game

Putting is a game of pace and line: without good pace and good line you will never hole a putt. Some golfers have great direction control but terrible distance control or vice versa. Here are a few tips and a great game to help improve your speed.

'Find the stroke'. Before you take any putt I want you to find the stroke that will hole that putt. You may need to make 2 or 3 practice strokes to find the stroke. When you think that you've found the stroke, set up to the golf ball and repeat that exact stroke on the ball. Providing you have aligned yourself correctly to the hole and proving you found the correct speed there's no reason why you should ever miss. A great way to practise your distance control is with your eyes closed. Focus on the target to begin with, have your practice strokes, then close your eyes and repeat the practice stroke on the ball.

(39, 40, 41) I have measured a circle around a golf hole and I have marked the circle using tee pegs. I have measured each tee peg a putter's length from the hole (just under 3 feet). I will now position myself a good distance away from the hole. For this demonstration I have positioned myself 15 paces away from the hole, approximately 45 feet. My goal is to roll all six of my golf balls inside the circle.

I am trying to find the stroke, I have looked at the hole, and now I am having three rehearsal strokes to try and find the correct stroke for the job in hand (42, 43).

As you can see, I'm not doing too badly (44, 45, 46). The first putt is so important. You can gain so much from that first putt. I want you to test yourself with the distance putts. Use six balls to begin with, start off from 10 paces and keep increasing the distance. You should be able to get all six balls inside the circle from any distance when you have mastered this exercise.

Remember: same speed back and through, same distance back and through, stay still. The longer the putt the longer the stroke.

Greenside bunkers

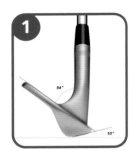

What do I do? Don't panic!

The main objective when we find ourselves in a greenside bunker is to get the ball out first time. In order to do this you don't necessarily have to hit the ball. Blast the sand and the ball out of the bunker together without actually making contact with the golf ball. How do you do this? Read on!

Characteristics of the Sand Wedge

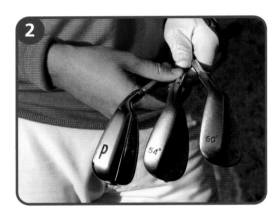

What club do I play?

There are certain factors to take into consideration when it comes to club selection with the bunker shots: distance, texture of sand (deep, soft and fluffy or hard, shallow and compact) and also the face of the bunker.

Understand the bounce angle – this is the measurement taken from the ground to the bottom of the club face (1): the higher this angle the less it will dig into the sand, the lower the angle the more it will dig in.

Here I have selected three clubs that I would use for greenside bunker shots: Pitching Wedge, Sand Wedge and Lob Wedge (2). Let me show you how to be smart with your club selection.

The Pitching Wedge

This has the least loft of the three. My Pitching Wedge has 47 degrees of loft. This club would be ideal if I was faced with a longer bunker shot or if the sand is compacted. Due to the 47 degrees of loft the ball will come out slightly lower, therefore travelling further. The angle between the bottom edge of the club and the sole (the bounce) is 8 degrees, allowing the club to dig into the sand enabling me to get underneath the ball. This would be a good choice for a longer greenside bunker shot if the sand was slightly compacted.

The Sand Wedge

This is the club I would choose for greenside bunker shots. My Sand Wedge has 54 degrees of loft and has 10 degrees of bounce. This means that it will get the ball reasonably high and will be good in soft to regular sand. It wouldn't however be too good if the sand was hard and compact. A standard Sand Wedge has 56 degrees of loft, but players nowadays will vary the loft to suit their game and also to complement their set of clubs.

The Lob Wedge

I would use this club when I have got a short bunker shot, or if I want the ball to go higher. My Lob Wedge has 60 degrees of loft, sending the ball high. It only has 4 degrees of bounce. I would not be using this club if the sand was deep and fluffy because of the lack of bounce – the Lob Wedge would dig in too much, therefore slowing the club head down and probably leaving the ball in the bunker.

How do I play the shot?

Open up the club face – Notice how I have opened the club face (club face aiming right) a fraction and gripped the club in its open position (3).

Opening the club face will assist in getting the ball out nice and high and will prevent the club digging down. If the club face is in a square position at impact the club will dig into the sand. If the club face is in a closed position then it would dig in too much, leaving the ball in the bunker. Opening the club face will bounce the sole of the club in and then straight back out of the sand causing a sand and ball explosion.

It's important to understand what I mean by grip the club in an open (aiming to the right) position. I want you to turn the club head slightly, approximately 45 degrees. Once you have turned the club head I then want you to grip the club in this position. It's really important that you don't grip it normally and then just rotate your forearms as this will cause the club face to return in a square, not open, position.

Top Tip – Use a slightly weaker grip (hands to the left) and this will encourage the club face to open through impact. The last thing I want is my hands rotating, as this will close the club face.

Stand wide for a firm base – To be a good bunker player you must obtain a wide base. The greenside bunker shot requires tremendous balance so a wide solid base is required. Notice how my feet are just a little wider than my shoulders. My knees are flexed and my lower half is firm, and this will help maintain my balance (4).

Open up the body – I've now gripped the golf club so now it's time to position my body. My club face is currently aiming way to the right of the target (5). If I was to just go ahead and hit the shot from here – well, there's no prize for guessing where it's going to go. Notice how I've walked my body to the left until my club face is pointing to the target (6). My body is now aiming to the left of the target, and my feet, knees, hips and shoulders are completely in line and pointing to the left of the target. However, the all-important club face is pointing directly at the target.

Greenside Bunkers

Do the shuffle and lean left

It's essential to keep good balance to be a good bunker player. I also want the golf club to travel underneath the ball. Once I have opened up my body and the club face is aiming at the target, I am going to shuffle my feet into the sand to help with my balance and also lower me slightly into the sand (7). Notice how I am leaning to the left and have positioned my body weight so it's favouring the left side 60/40 (8). This will encourage me to strike down into the sand, allowing the club to travel underneath the ball and explode the ball out.

Position that ball

Notice how the ball is positioned slightly forward in the stance (9). This is because I intend to strike the sand before the ball. The lowest point of the arc of the golf swing is underneath my chin. This is where the club is going to enter the sand. Positioning the ball forward will help me strike the sand before the ball.

Where do I hit the sand?

It all depends on the length of the shot or how you want the ball to roll when it lands on the green. Generally, you should stick to the 2-inch, 1-inch rule. For the majority of the greenside bunker shots you should intend to strike the sand approximately 2 inches behind the ball (10). If you have a slightly longer bunker shot or if you want to spin the ball, then you should intend to strike the sand approximately 1 inch behind the ball. To be so precise in striking the sand behind the ball you must focus on a grain of sand behind the ball. You can see here I have placed a tee peg into the sand, and this is a great way to practise this shot (11). Stare at the tee peg and concentrate on hitting the tee before you hit the ball (12). This is where your set-up and balance need to be good.

Swing across and blast – One great technique is to swing across the line of your toes (swing to the left). Swinging left with the open club face will pop the ball straight up in the air. Don't be shy when playing the shot – accelerate the club through the hitting area, and blast both the sand and the ball out of the bunker, then watch it finish close to the hole (13, 14, 15, 16, 17, 18)!

The actual golf swing is dominated by the top half of your body – shoulders, arms and hands; the lower half must remain solid throughout.

TOP TIPS:

- *Stare at the point where you intend the club to enter the sand approximately 1 - 2 inches behind the ball.*
- *Keep the body weight left-sided. Don't transfer the weight.*
- *Keep your wrists firm.*
- *Swing the club across the line of the feet.*
- *Feel your left hand pulling through the shot.*
- *Accelerate the golf club through impact.*
- *Blast the sand and the ball out of the bunker. Don't be shy!*

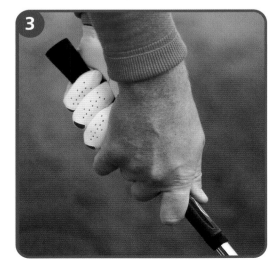

Fairway bunkers

To improve your game from the fairway bunker I want you to ask yourself a number of questions.

How is the ball sitting?

Can I reach the green?

How far do I have to reach the green?

What club will it take to reach the green?

Can I comfortably clear the face of the bunker with the chosen club?
(This is probably the most important question of all).

If you are 100 per cent sure that you can clear the lip of the bunker then go ahead and play the shot. If you are not so sure then you may need to consider the lay up shot.

I see so many players attempting the Hollywood shot (very risky but looks good) from fairway bunkers. It's great when it comes off but it can be very costly and you do look foolish if you hit the shot straight into the face of the bunker and the ball then rolls down the face and finishes up where it started from.

I'm not saying that you must always use your most lofted club – what I am saying is be smart. You often see tour professionals using fairway woods out of the bunker. This is fine if the ball is sitting up, the face is low and the sand is compact, and above all you are confident.

Escape that hazard (1)

The biggest obstacle is to clear the lip when playing the fairway bunker shot.

How do I do it?

When playing from a fairway bunker the idea is to strike the ball without touching the sand, unlike the greenside bunker shot. If any sand should get in between the ball and the club face, then it would take a great deal of speed away. I tend to grip a fraction further down the shaft and take one extra club.

At address I want you to position the ball slightly back in the stance as this will help crisp up your strikes. Your stance should be the same width as for a normal shot. You can see that my feet are approximately shoulder-width apart here (2). A strong footing is needed. Shuffle your feet into the sand to get a good grip before you make the swing. I am going to be making a full golf swing from sand so I can't afford to slip.

I want you to grip just a fraction further down the handle and grip the club slightly tighter (3). Gripping the club tighter will assist with a wider swing that has very little wrist movement and will promote a much shallower angle of attack, so you can pick the ball off cleanly without taking too much sand.

Chin up – when picking the ball off the top of the sand cleanly you must keep your height throughout the swing. When addressing the golf ball you should have your chin up high and peer down at the ball (4).

(5, 6, 7, 8, 9, 10, 11) My thought for this swing is to stay tall and think '80 per cent'. I would always use an extra club to take these factors into consideration. My impact position is almost identical to my address position and I have kept standing tall throughout the swing. Notice I have held a nice high finish position, with the club shaft at the back of my neck, and all of my body weight is now on my left side. I know I have made a good swing if I can hold a balanced position here. Hold the pose and watch the ball finish next to the pin.

Awkward Lies

Golf is such a great game because no two golf courses are the same; they all have their own characteristics. Some of the world's greatest golf courses rely on the natural slope of the land, and are often in beautiful settings. Golf would be boring if every course was the same.

When you are a beginner and you get bitten by the golfing bug you will generally head for the local driving range and perhaps have a lesson with a PGA professional. You will learn to hit the golf ball and how to build your swing. All of this is done from a completely flat piece of ground. When you head out to the golf course you will notice that apart from the teeing ground, most golf courses are anything but flat!

Here is some great advice to help you conquer the sloping lies and better yourself as golfer.

There are mainly five different positions that you will generally find yourself in on the golf course, and I would like to highlight these positions:

1. the flat lie
2. the uphill lie
3. the downhill lie
4. the 'ball above the level of your feet' lie
5. the 'ball below the level of your feet' lie.

In this section I am going to concentrate on the four awkward lies that you will no doubt be faced with at some point on the golf course.

The ups and downs

The uphill lie

When your ball is on an uphill slope there are a number of key points that you need to be aware of. The ball will obviously fly higher and therefore it is not going to travel as far, so you will have to club up (1). So, for example, if you are a 6-iron distance away and you find your ball on an uphill slope, you will have to use more club, maybe a 4-iron. The club change obviously depends on the severity of the slope.

The ball will not only fly high from this position but it will also have a tendency to fly from right to left with draw/hook spin. This is because it's very difficult to transfer your body weight, as you end up hanging back on your right side then your hands and arms take over, closing the club face and promoting the right-to-left spin.

(2, 3) Stand on the slope. When addressing the ball I want you to position your spine at right angles to the slope. This means that your body weight will now be slightly favouring the right side.

Don't lean in to the slope as this will restrict your back swing and you'll find it hard to control the flight.

Notice how the ball is positioned in the centre of my stance. If I play the ball forward, the club face is likely to close because my body is less active due to the uphill slope. I could also run the risk of hitting a fat (ground before the ball) shot. Be smart, play it in the middle!

The stance is just slightly wider than normal. This is to ensure that balance is kept throughout the golf swing. The more severe the slope the wider you should stand.

I have placed a club on the ground to demonstrate how you need to align your body (4). Due to the uphill slope the ball will fly from right to left, so I have aimed fractionally to the right of the target to allow for the right-to-left flight.

(5, 6, 7, 8) The back swing will appear to be shorter; this is only because my spine is now tilted behind the ball, giving the impression that the swing is short. When making the golf swing you will feel that it's very difficult to get all of your body weight on to the left side and hold the follow-through. Try to hold the full finish as best you can to achieve a straighter flight. If you hang your body weight back you will run the risk of hitting the ground before the ball and also hitting the big hook (right to left).

Awkward Lies

Downhill lie

As you might expect, this is completely the opposite of the uphill lie – the ball is going to fly lower and further. The ball is likely to fly with fade/slice spin (left to right), because the swing will be more upright and across the ball. Your lower half will become more active as you swing through, so don't hit too hard and try to stay in balance.

(1) You will have to select a more lofted golf club when faced with this shot. The distance needed here suggests a 6-iron but due to the slope that I have I am now going to use the 8-iron. The change of club will depend on the severity of the slope.

Position your body weight at right angles to the slope. Your weight will now be favouring the left side.

The golf ball should be positioned slightly forward of centre. This is because when striking the ball your lower half will become quite active so it is easy to get too far ahead of the ball causing a push to the right. Moving the ball forward will help prevent the push.

If you are faced with an extreme slope, play the ball from the centre of your stance to avoid striking the ground behind.

The golf ball will have a tendency to fly to the right because the swing is now more upright, so when addressing the golf ball I want you to aim a fraction to the left of the target. The steeper the slope, the further left you should aim.

The stance is wider to help promote good balance throughout.

(2,3,4) A good thought to have when taking this shot is "swing down the slope" and this will prevent you hitting upwards on the ball.

Stay in control by easing up a little: think '80 per cent' and this will ensure that you keep your balance throughout. You will notice that I have held my body shape throughout my back swing, and I am completely in balance.

When striking the golf ball you will find that your legs become more active during the swing – this is due to the slope. At this point the wider stance will help.

Side hill lies

Ball above the level of your feet

The first thing I want you to understand is that when the ball is above your feet, your club face will point to the left of the target. This is because the lie angle has now changed. The more lofted the club the more it will aim to the left.

The golf swing will also become more rounded as a result of the slope. The more rounded swing will again cause the golf ball to fly to the left, due to the club face closing at impact.

The ball will have a tendency to fly slightly further because of the club face closing and producing the draw spin, so you may want to take one less club for this shot.

The ball is now much closer to your eyes and body, and this is why you need to grip further down the club (1). If I gripped the club so it is at full length I would run the risk of hitting a heavy shot (the ground before the ball).

When standing to the ball (2), make sure your body weight is on the balls of your feet. If you let your weight fall back on your heels this will promote an even more rounded golf swing and you will also risk losing balance.

Align yourself to the right of the target; how far to the right depends on the severity of the slope.

Position the ball in the centre of your stance. If you play the ball forward, this will send the ball to the left. If you are faced with a severe slope, move the ball back a fraction to counteract the pull to the left.

You will notice that I'm standing taller although I am still bending forward from my hips. If you stand with your spine vertical (too tall) the back swing will become far too rounded, making it impossible to judge the direction, and will affect the strike.

(3, 4, 5) A great swing thought to have with this one is "keep your height – stay in your spine angle". It's very easy to lose your height when playing this shot. Notice that my spine angle has stayed absolutely the same throughout the golf swing.

Complete the through-swing and stay in balance. It's very easy to allow your hands and arms to take over.

Try to achieve a full follow-through position, as this will prevent the big hook (extreme left to right).

Awkward Lies

Ball below the level of your feet

When the ball is positioned below your feet it will have a tendency to move to the right with fade/slice spin. This is because of two factors:

1. When the club is at a more upright angle the club face points will aim to the right; the more loft on the club, the more it will aim to the right.

2. The golf swing will become steeper. When striking the ball, the club will strike slightly across the ball, resulting in left-to-right spin.

The golf swing will be dominated by the upper body. This is because the lower half of the body is acting more as a support than as a dynamic part of the swing.

Be aware, though, that the steeper the slope, the more the heel (closest part to the shaft) can dig into the ground causing the club head to close, resulting in the hook.

Try to grip the club at its full length (1). Do not try to extend the club by gripping right at the tip, as this will result in loss of control, resulting in inconsistent strikes and wayward shots.

Aim to the left of the target because the ball is likely to move to the right; how far you should aim to the left depends on the severity of the slope (2).

You will notice that the golf ball is further away from my eyes and body than normal. When addressing the ball, make sure that your body weight is on the balls of your feet; do not sit back on your heels as this will result in hitting the ground before you hit the ball. Do not lean your weight too far forward on your toes as this will result in loss of balance.

Try to raise your hands a fraction to get the sole of the club flat on the ground; this will prevent the heel of the golf club digging in and closing the club face.

Flex your knees more for this shot and try to make your stance a bit wider; this will bring you lower and thus closer to the golf ball, making it easier to strike the ball.

(3, 4, 5, 6) The key thought for the swing here is 'stay down through the shot'; this will often result in losing your balance after impact but you must try to keep your body down throughout the follow-through. Golfers find this shot particularly difficult, because they are eager to see where the ball has gone. If you straighten up prior to impact, this will lead to top shots and thins (striking the ball half way up and across the ground).

Notice that my spine angle has remained the same throughout the golf swing. The golf swing itself appears to be slightly shorter, but this is because the lower body is held still while the upper body makes the swing.

Stay in balance – try to maintain your balance in the follow-through for this shot.

With all of the awkward lies it is important that you follow my tips. Have lots of practice 'rehearsal swings' before you play the shot, as this will give you a good idea of how the slope will affect your golf swing.

TOP TIPS

- *See the shot before you play the shot – what will happen?*
- *Take time and carefully select your club.*
- *Never aim directly at the target, because with all of these shots the ball will curve in different directions.*
- *Stay in posture throughout the swing.*
- *From uphill and downhill, swing along the contours of the slope.*
- *Make practice swings to start.*

Awkward Bunkers

In an ideal world, when you hit your ball into a bunker you would always find a completely flat, nicely prepared lie in the sand. Unfortunately, in real life this rarely happens. When you are out on the course you will certainly be faced with some awkward situations in the bunkers. I want you to have the know-how to be able to escape from the bunker when you are faced with an awkward lie. I am going to describe two of the most common problems that you will be faced with when experiencing the 'delights' of bunker play.

The most common of the awkward bunker shots is the 'plugged lie' (1). This is where the golf ball comes down from a great height and embeds itself deep into the bunker. If you are playing a course with deep sand in the bunkers then you will surely be faced with this shot at some point. This is a very difficult shot to play because to get the ball out you need to make a huge sand explosion. Lots of sand gets between the club face and the ball, so it's impossible to control the spin on the golf ball. The ball will come out of the bunker with very little spin, and thus when it lands on the green it will roll more than usual.

How do I play the plugged lie?

When playing this shot the club needs to go in deep! To get the ball out of the plugged lie you need power. This is not the time for those elegant swings – you need to select the club that will dig in. As I explained in the greenside bunker section, different wedges have different bounce angles, so if you have a Sand Wedge with a lot of bounce then this is not the club for this shot; perhaps choose the Pitching Wedge or even a Lob Wedge. There are obviously different severities of the plugged lie. I explained in the greenside bunker instructions that you need to open the club face, but when playing the plugged lie this is not always the case.

Notice how I closed the club face (2). I know that this is completely the opposite of what was shown for the greenside bunker, but this is a method that works! When you close the club face, as it strikes the sand the bottom edge of the club will act like a knife, digging down underneath the ball, and this is exactly what you want for this shot. I want you now to position your body completely square to the target. When you strike down into the sand the force of the sand will open the club face as it travels under the ball, sending the ball up and out of the bunker.

The body weight is positioned even more so to the left side (70/30); notice how my shoulders are almost level with the sand at this point, because my body weight is so far forward. My stance is a little wider for this shot and my knees are flexed. This brings me lower and will help send the club face under the ball.

I have fixed my wrists earlier for this shot which will help strike down behind the ball with great speed. The body weight is still on the front foot, with absolutely no weight transference here.

At impact, I want you to feel that you are striking the sand approximately 2 inches behind the ball (3). Stare at this point throughout the swing.

Don't peek to see if you've made it! Keep staring at the spot and accelerate the club through the shot (4). When the through-swing is complete, then you can look and admire the results.

The Uphill Bunker Shot

The majority of greenside bunkers have a steep face to them, which makes them that little bit more difficult. You need to know how to play the shot when your ball lies at the face of the bunker. The ball will fly higher due to the added loft on the club, so club selection again is vital. If you have a long bunker shot, rather than swing harder, club down and choose perhaps a Pitching Wedge or even a 9-iron.

With all bunker shots, balance is the key (5). This is certainly the case with this shot. Notice how I have adopted a much wider stance here. You must maintain your posture when playing this shot. Standing wide will hold me steady. My body weight is set on my back foot for this shot, due to the slope. My right foot is going to act as my support. If you lean into the slope, you will run the risk of picking up far too much sand and hit the ball straight into the face of the bunker.

At address, I want you to stand at right angles to the slope of the bunker (6). The ball is still positioned slightly forward in my stance and I am still staring at that same point 2 inches behind the ball.

When making the golf swing I want you to hold your set-up position (7, 8). This swing is all about the arms and hands; your body really doesn't do anything apart from providing support throughout.

Shape It!

I am fully aware that golfers spend the majority of their time trying to hit the ball in a straight line, but sometimes straight is not what you need. When you look at some of the best players in the world they have the ability to shape the flight of the golf ball from right to left and left to right. If you can master these shots you will find the game so much easier, and it will allow you to go for the green on occasions, rather than chipping out on to the fairway. You will make golf holes play shorter if you can shape your ball around a dogleg. You will also become a better golfer in the wind if you can shape your shots into the wind, preventing it from blowing your ball off course.

To achieve this, you will need to have a good understanding of how the swing path affects the flight of your ball, this will help to fine-tune your own golf swing.

In this section I am going to show you how to hit the ball from right to left (the hook), left to right (the fade) and also the highs and the lows.

The fade or slice (left to right)

A fade is when the ball starts off to the left of the target and then moves back to the right and heads for the target. The slice is an exaggerated fade, when the ball moves severely from left to right.

To hit the fade or slice the golf club must cut across the ball with a glancing blow, creating the left to right spin. The club face must remain open throughout the hitting area – closing the clubface would result in a pull to the left.

For the average golfer this is probably an easier shot to master, because most players hit at the ball with their upper body, creating a steeper swing path that moves across the ball, resulting in the left to right spin.

You can see what I am faced with here (1). I have tall pine trees directly in line with my golf ball and this obstacle is too high to go over. I want to slice the ball around the trees and on to the green.

(2) The first thing you need to do if you want to hit the fade/slice is to open the club face (club aiming to the right). When opening the club face I don't want you to merely rotate your forearms, I want you to grip the golf club in an open position.

Hitting the golf shot with an open club face will send the ball slightly higher, so you will have to use an extra club or two when playing this shot. Therefore, if you are a 7-iron distance away from the target, then you should use a 6-iron or even a 5-iron, the reason being that when you fade the ball, you open the club face and as a result hit the ball slightly higher and not as far.

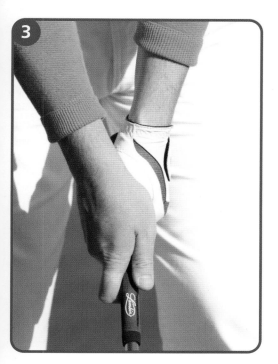

I've gripped the golf club in an open position but I have also adopted a slightly weaker grip (hands further to the right) (3). By weakening the grip when striking the ball you can be sure that the club face will remain open at impact. Be aware that the more you weaken your grip, the higher the ball will fly.

The club on the ground is following the ball-to-target line (4). When hitting the fade/slice, you must align your body to the left of the target. Notice how my feet, knees, hips and shoulders are pointing to the left of the target. The club face, however, is pointing directly towards the target.

The ball position should be slightly further forward in your stance. This will encourage the out to in (right to left) path of the swing that we need to hit the fade (5).

Shape It

Swing Sequences (6, 7, 8, 9, 10, 11)

When making the golf swing I want you to feel as if your upper body alone performs the movement. At impact, feel as if your shoulders are in an open (pointing left) position. Notice how I am swinging the golf club to the left. The golf swing should also be slightly steeper (more upright) to encourage the slice spin.

I am holding the club face open until the follow-through is completed. I do not want the club face to rotate at any point. The follow-through is slightly shorter and the club head is pointing to the sky. This is a good sign that the club face remained open throughout the swing, and the ball should travel from left to right.

The draw or hook (right to left)

A draw is when the golf ball starts to move to the right of the target and then swings back to the left. A hook is when the golf ball starts to move to the right and curves viciously to the left.

This is a very strong flighted shot. It is often said that the draw shot goes further than the fade. Many people think it is something to do with the spin and that the right-to-left spin will travel further than one from left to right. The truth is that when you draw the ball, the club face closes (rotates) through impact. There is far less loft on the club and the right-to-left spin is generated with less back spin; as a result the ball will fly lower and further. With the fade the club face is open, thus sending the ball higher, generating more left-to-right spin and more back spin, but losing distance.

The draw is definitely the harder shot of the two to master. If you usually fade the golf ball and you would like to learn how to draw the ball instead, read on – this will definitely help.

Here I'm playing a hole that dog-legs (bends) from right to left. My golf ball has unfortunately found the left side of the fairway and I am completely blocked out by the trees (12). My options are to chip out or go for it by hitting a big slinging hook, from right to left, that finds the green.

Close the club face

When closing the club face, the ball will want to fly to the left (13). It will also fly further, so remember to take less club when attempting this shot.

Shape It

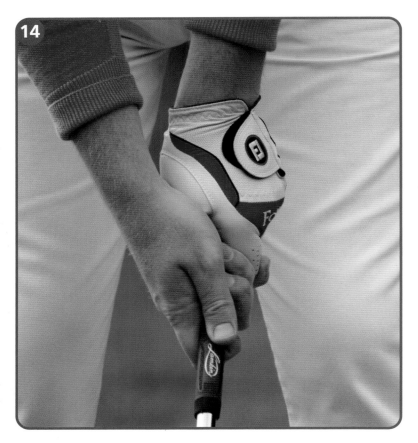

Stronger grip

A stronger grip doesn't mean holding the club tighter, it means moving the hands to the right side of the grip. You can see that most of my knuckles are visible on my left hand, and my right hand is also slightly further underneath the grip (14).

Make sure you grip the club in a closed position, don't just rotate your forearms.

The reason for gripping the club this way is to close the club face when releasing it. As a result, when striking the golf ball the hands will want to return to a neutral position, thus closing the club and spinning the ball from right to left.

The aim

I have placed a club on the ground to indicate where the line of the target is. The club face should remain pointing to the target during the set-up. My feet, knees, hips and shoulders are pointing to the right of the target, in a closed position (15).

Ball position

The ball is positioned slightly back in my stance. This is because the swing will strike the ball in an inside to outside path; it also makes me keep my shoulders slightly closed. It is not advisable, when playing the draw/hook, to play the ball forward in the stance.

In this picture it appears that the ball is a long way back in my stance. This is merely because I am aiming to the right and the picture is taken head-on to the target. The ball should be just back from centre to play this shot (16).

Swing Sequences (17, 18, 19, 20, 21)

For this shot the golf swing needs to be more rounded. This is to help promote an in-to-out swing path. I am actually hitting the golf ball out to the right and allowing the set-up to do the work.

Top Tip: Stay down through impact and feel your right hand working over the top. Think of a top spin shot in tennis.

The adjustments made in the set-up will cause the golf ball to draw/hook; we are just adding some extras to make sure it bends.

With this shot I am playing an extreme hook, so you will notice that the through-swing is quite rounded. This is because I have really whipped my right hand over the ball, achieving my hook.

If I were playing a nice quiet draw shot, then I wouldn't close the club face so much. I would stand squarer to the ball and I would try to maintain a nice high finish, feeling the golf club coming from an inside to out.

Introduction

When you are out on your local golf course or perhaps in the bar at the clubhouse, don't you find yourself, on occasion, chatting to your fellow competitors or friends about how you would love to play golf on some exotic course in some wonderful far-off country? Well, perhaps it isn't so far away. Let's face it, the world has shrunk a great deal in the past ten years, when it comes to travelling. Whereas previously the USA and Australia were considered to be too far away, and too expensive to get to, today it's often just a matter of finding the time in your busy life.

This chapter of the book is here to tempt you with some mouthwatering places you might like to consider visiting to play that ultimate round of golf. From the bonnie wee banks of Loch Lomond in Scotland, to the exotic sands of Dubai, it's all here. The USA without doubt is a favourite for golfers and has some of the most breathtaking courses in the world, but you could also just pit yourself against the wind and terrain of the original home of golf, St Andrews. At the least, a pilgrimage to where it all started has to be on the cards.

Read on and I defy you to say no to all the wonderful courses we have featured. There surely has to be one you would like to visit!

Augusta National, USA

Cypress Point, USA

Oakmont, USA

Pebble Beach Golf Links, USA

Pine Valley, USA

Pinehurst No.2, USA

Sawgrass, USA

Shinnecock Hills, USA

Royal Birkdale, England

Sunningdale, England

Wentworth, England

Woodhall Spa, England

Carnoustie, Scotland

Loch Lomond, Scotland

Muirfield, Scotland

Royal Dornoch, Scotland

St Andrews Old Course, Scotland

Turnberry Ailsa Championship Course, Scotland

Celtic Manor Twenty Ten, Wales

Ballybunion, Eire

Royal County Down, N Ireland

Royal Portrush, N Ireland

Emirates, UAE

Kingston Heath, Australia

New South Wales, Australia

Royal Melbourne, Australia

Cape Kidnappers, New Zealand

Durban Country Club, S Africa

Hirono, Japan

Valderrama, Spain

Augusta National USA

Augusta National Golf Club is located in Augusta, Georgia, USA and is one of the most famous and exclusive golf clubs in the world. It was founded by Bobby Jones on the site of a former indigo plantation, and the club opened for play in January 1933. Since 1934 it has played host to the annual Masters Tournament, one of the four major championships in professional golf.

Uniquely, each hole on the course is named after the tree or shrub with which it has become associated. For example, number one is the Olive Tree, number two is Dogwood and the last, number 18, is named Holly, and so forth.

Most players will agree that it is the 14th hole that is the most difficult to play. The greatest challenge of this hole is to place the ball as close to the pin as possible. Not an easy task, taking into consideration the undulating green.

Several architectural features should be mentioned. A structure known as the Crow's Nest is made available for amateurs who want to be housed there during the Masters Tournament. The Eisenhower Cabin, one of ten cabins, was built by the club's

Rae's Creek cuts across the south-eastern corner of the Augusta course and flows along the back of the 11th green, in front of the 12th green, and ahead of the 13th tee. The Hogan and Nelson Bridges cross the creek after the 12th and 13th tee boxes, respectively. The creek was named after former property owner John Rae, who died in 1789.

membership for President Dwight D Eisenhower. There is a memorial located in front of the course's clubhouse, at the end of Magnolia Lane, with a plaque which honours Bobby Jones and Clifford Roberts. A bridge over Rae's Creek, covered with artificial turf, that connects the fairway of hole 12 to its green was dedicated to Ben Hogan in 1958 to commemorate his 72-hole score of 274 strokes five years earlier, the course record at the time. The main driveway leading to the clubhouse is flanked on either side by 61 magnolia trees and is appropriately named Magnolia Lane. A stonework bridge over Rae's Creek that connects the teeing ground of hole 13 to its fairway was dedicated in 1958 to Byron Nelson, to honour his performance in the 1937 Masters. The par 3 Fountain, situated next to the number one tee on the par 3 course, has a list of par 3 contest winners, starting with Sam Snead's win in 1960. The Record Fountain was built to commemorate the 25th anniversary of the Masters and is located left of the number 17 tee; it displays course records and Masters Tournament champions. A bridge over the pond on hole 15 that separates the fairway from the green was named for Gene Sarazen, for a memorable double eagle in the 1935 Masters Tournament that propelled him to victory.

A beautiful aerial view of the course's clubhouse. The lane leading to it is flanked on either side by 61 magnolia trees, each grown from seeds planted by the Berckman family in the 1850s. There is also a memorial in front of it to Bobby Jones and Clifford Roberts.

General Eisenhower, as he was then known, returned from a walk through the woods on the eastern part of the Augusta grounds, and informed Clifford Roberts that he had found a perfect place to build a dam for a fish pond. The pond, named Ike's Pond, after the President, was built and located just where he wanted it.

Course Specifications

Location:	Augusta, Georgia, USA
Established:	1933
Type:	Private
Total holes:	18
Designed by:	Alister MacKenzie
Par:	72
Length:	7,445 yards

89

Cypress Point USA

Known around the world for its series of three breathtaking holes – 15th, 16th and 17th – that run adjacent to the Pacific Ocean, Cypress Point Golf Club is an 18-hole course positioned on the beautiful California coastline near Monterey, USA. Many will argue that the 16th hole is the best golf hole in the world and without doubt it is impressive. The final 18th hole was never completed to the designer's specification; it was intended to have the tee dramatically perched on a rock sitting out in the ocean, with a suspension bridge for access.

The course, one of several, was formerly used to hold the AT&T Pebble Beach National Pro-Am and did so for the last time in 1991. This is a private members' club, and so the opportunity to play this spectacular course is restricted to the small number of elite members and the guests they might invite.

The breathtaking Cypress Point Golf course, running adjacent to the rugged Pacific Ocean coastline.

A view of the 16th hole taken during the AT&T Pebble Beach Pro-Am competition in 1988. Many players will tell you that this is the best golf hole in the world, and there seems little reason to dispute that statement.

Players at the first hole during the AT&T Pebble Beach Pro-Am tournament in 1991. The well-appointed clubhouse can be seen in the background between the cypress trees.

Course Specifications

Location:	Pebble Beach, California, USA
Established:	1928
Type:	Private
Total holes:	18
Designed by:	Alister MacKenzie
Par:	72
Length:	6,524 yards

Oakmont USA

The first US golf club to be designed as a national historic Landmark, Oakmont nestles in the rolling hills outside Pittsburgh, Pennsylvania and is often ranked amongst the top 5 golf courses in America. It is well known for its extremely fast greens, thick rough, and the turf-laden bunker between the third and fourth holes known as the church pews.

This bunker was made up of seven parallel bunkers, each separated by a high ridge of grass, which have been part of Oakmont since its early days. It was during the U.S. Open in 1935 that the bunkers were wrapped around the ridges to connect with each other, creating the now famous 'Church Pew Bunker'.

Regarded by many as the toughest course in America, the greens have changed little since the course was designed around 100 years ago. For example, the 456- yard 18th hole has been described by many golfers as the best par 4 in golf, although the 482-yard, par 4 opening hole has its claim to fame too – it was voted the PGA Tour's most difficult hole.

The Tudor-style clubhouse at Oakmont Country Club is full of history and could tell a few stories. It has been the backdrop to so many US Open tournaments, and its twin gabled roofs have been seen so many times on television that they are nearly as famous as the 'Church Pew' bunkers.

Looking very much as it did when it was first built, the Oakmont clubhouse is a two-storey Tudor style building. Restoration was carried out between 2002 and 2007, with much attention paid to keeping the original feel of the building. Although structural and mechanical components have been upgraded, things like spike marks in the locker room have been retained, along with old photographs of past tournaments. There is a whole wall dedicated to the 1962 US Open playoff between Jack Nicklaus and Arnold Palmer.

Besides hosting many other tournaments, Oakmont has been selected as host for the US Open eight times (1927, 1935, 1953, 1962, 1973, 1983, 1994 and 2007), which is more than any other course.

These are the famous 'Church Pew' bunkers, which have brought many a player to their knees for a quick prayer.

Course Specifications

Location:	Oakmont, Pennsylvania, USA
Established:	1903
Type:	Private
Total holes:	18
Designed by:	Henry Fownes
Par:	71
Length:	7,255 yards

Pebble Beach Golf Links USA

Pebble Beach Golf Links, widely regarded as the most beautiful course in the world, is one of several golf courses in Pebble Beach, California, and possibly the most famous in the western United States.

Using a figure-of-eight layout, the designers had one objective: that was to place as many holes alongside the rugged and beautiful Monterey peninsular as possible, and they succeeded handsomely.

The last hole is a medium-length par 5 and has an incredible Pacific Ocean backdrop. What many would describe as the greatest closing hole in golf, the 18th was originally an unremarkable par 4 until 1922, when William Herbert Fowler added an extra 200 yards or so. There is also a tree in the middle of the fairway with a long 100 yard-plus bunker running along the ocean from the green.

The exquisite beauty and unique challenge of Pebble Beach Golf Links have thrilled golfers and spectators alike since 1919. In this aerial view the spectacular 7th hole can clearly be admired.

Just recently an extra piece of land, which was sold off in the early days of the course, has been re-acquired. On this strip of land Jack Nicklaus designed a new par 3, which, although leaving a long walk from the 5th green to the 6th tee, allows the course to use as much of the ocean frontage as possible, which conforms to the designers' original intentions.

To pick one memorable hole at Pebble Beach Links would be difficult, but the 8th is notable in that not only is it one of the most photographed holes in golf, but from an elevated tee, players hit the ball straight out to sea, towards an often violent Pacific surf thundering against the rocks. The long par 3 17th hole booked its place in golf history when in 1972 Jack Nicklaus, and just ten years later Tom Watson, made key shots there to win the US Open.

This is the incredibly beautiful Monterey peninsula on the California coast, where Pebble Beach Golf Links is located.

Course Specifications

Location:	Pebble Beach, California, USA
Established:	1919
Total holes:	18
Designed by:	Jack Neville and Douglas Grant
Par:	72
Length:	6,828 yards

Pine Valley USA

Regularly ranked the number one course in *Golf Digest's* list of America's 100 greatest courses, Pine Valley Golf Club is situated in Pine Valley, New Jersey.

A group of amateur golfers from Philadelphia purchased 184 acres (0.7 km) of rolling, sandy ground deep in the pinelands of southern New Jersey. They put the responsibility for the design of this incredible golf course in the hands of George Arthur Crump, who knew the area from hunting expeditions he had made.

This would be his first and only golf course design, but he set himself some characteristic goals. There would be no hole laid out parallel to the next; no more than two consecutive holes should play in the same direction; and players should not be able to see any hole other than the one they were playing. He also felt that a round of golf on his course should require a player to use every club in the bag.

Crump became obsessed with the project and decided to have marshlands drained and 22,000 tree stumps removed. He was so preoccupied with the design that the course even acquired the nickname of 'Crump Folly' at one stage.

A great view of the one-shot 5th, where the green is well elevated above its tee. A stream also runs between the tee and the green to make things a little trickier.

The first 11 holes were unofficially opened in 1914, soon after which Crump died, and by 1918, four holes were still incomplete. Since then many alterations have been made by other leading golf course designers.

Due to lack of spectator space, Pine Valley has never played host to any major professional tournament. In 1962 it did hold the Shell Wonderful World of Golf match between Gene Littler and Byron Nelson, and one day every year it allows the general public in to watch the Crump Cup, a nationally recognised tournament featuring elite mid-amateur players. 1936 and 1985 also saw the Walker Cup being played here.

Pine Valley is continually judged to be the finest course in the world, and has some interesting architectural features. It was the only course designed by George Arthur Crump.

Course Specifications

Location:	Pine Valley, New Jersey, USA
Established:	1913
Total holes:	18
Designed by:	George Arthur Crump
Par:	70
7Length:	6,999 yards

Pinehurst No.2 USA

James W Tufts sold his portion of the American Soda Fountain Company and made plans to create a health resort in the southeastern part of America. He purchased 5,500 acres of land in North Carolina and commissioned New York's Central Park designer Frederick Law Olmsted to design a village with winding streets and large open spaces. It was thus that Pinehurst was born.

The first clubhouse opened in 1898, and Doctor Le Roy Culver built Pinehurst's first nine-hole golf course. It was, however, Donald Ross's redesign that gave the course its wonderful character.

A second hotel, the Carolina, opened in 1901, the same year that America's longest-running amateur championship, the North and South, was inaugurated at Pinehurst.

No.2 course opened in 1902; it was also designed by Donald Ross, who continued to refine the course until his death in 1948. Although there are eight courses to choose from at Pinehurst, No.2 is the one on which everybody wants to be seen. It is regarded by many as the greatest golf course of all time, and was not only chosen to hold the 1999 and 2005 US Open Championships, but is due to host it again in 2014.

The 365-yard, par 4 13th hole, on the Pinehurst No 2 Course. This was the venue for the 2005 US Open Championship and it is also scheduled to hold it again in 2014.

The historic Pinehurst clubhouse is a building you will always remember, and rocking chairs strategically placed between the columns allow a wonderful view of the enormous putting green in front.

A combination of factors make Pinehurst No.2 a real challenge. Seen here is the green on the par 5 16th hole, with the par 3 17th hole just over on the right.

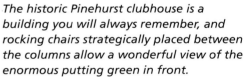

Course Specifications

Location:	Pinehurst, North Carolina, USA
Established:	1902
Total holes:	18
Designed by:	Donald Ross
Par:	72
Length:	7,305 yards

Sawgrass USA

The Stadium Course at Sawgrass in Florida has become one of the most famous courses in the world. It became the home of the PGA Tour and left people amazed at its architectural splendours.

Deane Beman, at the time commissioner of the PGA Tour, watched as the dream started to become a reality back in 1979. A 415-acre plot of soft marshland in northeast Florida would become the dream golf course, opening just a year later in 1980 as TPC Sawgrass. This was the first of many similar ventures which would make up the TPC network.

As amazing as it is, this is not just a course for the world's top players. It is a resort course and so is open as a daily-fee club, with amenities that will astound the visitor. Test yourself on one of golf's most renowned professional holes – the 132-yard par 3 17th hole, which, by the way, has an island green.

The Pete Dye-designed Players Stadium Course is home to one of the most challenging and photographed holes in the world, the famed 17th Island Green.

Part of the Tournament Players Clubs (TPC) network, which includes 23 facilities across the USA, this is one of eight courses that allow access to those who just love to play the game while indulging in the splendour of these magnificent courses and the facilities they offer. These top-class courses have been designed by the best contemporary architects – Tom Fazio, Bob Weed, Jack Nicklaus and Arnold Palmer, to name but a few. In each design, consideration is given to the environment and wildlife habitats that become part of the golf course.

A magnificent aerial view of the 17th island green, taken during the Thursday play-off during the Players Championship in 2006.

The 77,000-square feet, Mediterranean Revival-style clubhouse, pictured in May 2007 prior to the start of the Players Championship.

Course Specifications

Location:	Ponte Vedra, Florida, USA
Established:	1979
Type:	Public
Total holes:	18
Designed by:	Pete Dye
Par:	72
Length:	6,954 yards

Shinnecock Hills USA

Shinnecock Hills golf club was inspired by a trip made by William Vanderbilt, Duncan Cryder and Edward Mead while holidaying in France, where they first saw the game of golf being played. When they returned home to the USA, they decided to build a club in the Long Island town of Southampton.

And so it was that in 1891, with the technical assistance of Willie Davis, Royal Montreal Golf Club's professional, and some 150 Shinnecock Indians from the nearby reservation, a 12-hole course was constructed.

Two years later a nine-hole ladies-only course was built, and two years after that, in 1895, six more holes were designed and added to the original 12-hole course. Several improvements and redesigns were carried out over the years, including a major redesign when a highway cut the course in two.

Shinnecock has some unique aspects, for example the longer par 4s generally play downwind, whereas the shorter ones play into the wind, which when blowing comes from the southwest. Prominently sited on the top of a hill overlooking the course is the famous clubhouse, an iconic building that was designed by Stanford White.

The famous club house, designed by Stanford White, with the 9th hole in the foreground.

Shinnecock Hills has hosted the Open three times in modern times. 1986 saw Raymond Floyd win at the grand age of 43, in 1995 Corey Pavin took the honours and in 2004 Retief Goosen's putting skills secured him the title, while overcoming some of the worst conditions in the history of the US Open.

Today, Shinnecock Hills is seen as a prestigious, top ranking golf course and a major championship course. In 2007 it was placed second in *Golf Digest's* 100 Greatest Courses, and it is regularly at the top end of the league.

A birds-eye view of the course, taken just before the US Open in April 2003.

Course Specifications

Location:	Southampton, Long Island New York, USA
Established:	1891
Type:	Links
Total holes:	18
Designed by:	Willie Dunn
Par:	70
Length:	6,813 yards

Royal Birkdale England

The beginnings of the Royal Birkdale golf club go back to 30 July 1889, when nine gentlemen met to discuss the formation of a club, to be named Birkdale Golf Club. The discussion involved preparing a course and greens, hiring professionals and the provision of a clubhouse. It was agreed that 5 October would be the opening day, with the treasurer providing 'whisky and aerated waters' to celebrate.

Not long after it was agreed that ladies would be invited to use the links – a most unusual event – but only on three days a week and not on a Saturday or Bank Holiday. The original course had nine holes and was on Shaw Hills. In 1897 the club moved to the Birkdale Hills and a new 18-hole course was designed and constructed. Once again the ladies played a prominent part in the club.

1904 saw the building of a new permanent clubhouse overlooking what was then the 18th green. This would remain until 1935, when a new clubhouse was built and the course was remodelled ready for future championship tournaments.

The par 3 14th green is the last of the par 3s played from an elevated tee and is protected from the prevailing wind. Several deep greenside bunkers wait to collect a misdirected shot.

On 11 November 1951, the then captain of the club posted a notice announcing that His Majesty the King had 'been graciously pleased to Command that the Club shall henceforth be known as The Royal Birkdale Golf Club'.

During the 1960s, as golf became more popular as a spectator sport, the course and clubhouse once again went through changes. After the Open in 1991 the greens were completely dug up, redesigned and re-laid, which helped the Royal Birkdale to be voted the number one course by *Golf World* for 1998.

Today, Royal Birkdale is one of Britain's finest golf clubs and has been voted the number one course in the UK, and also ranks among the best in the world. It has hosted two Ryder Cups, the Walker and Curtis Cups, the Women's British Open and, on nine occasions, the Open Championship.

The clubhouse at Royal Birkdale, looking more like an old style airport building than a golf clubhouse, seen from the 479-yard par 4 18th hole.

Course Specifications

Location:	Southport, England
Established:	1889
Type:	Links
Total holes:	18
Designed by:	Fred Hawtree
Par:	71
Length:	7,018 yards

Sunningdale England

Sunningdale Golf Club held its first annual general meeting in 1900, and from then onwards its course has been re-worked and revised, causing many a quarrel. It is nonetheless a famous course, host to major championships.

The club was established on land leased from St John's College, Cambridge University, and was funded by a select group of financial contributors. In 1901, they erected a splendid clubhouse that follows the Edwardian style of verandas, turrets, and gables. An impressive clock adorns the front façade. During World War One, the lounge, the dining room and changing rooms were turned over to army use.

The original course, the 'Old Course', was designed by Willie Park Jnr, and in 1923 the New Course was created by Harry Colt. Both designers had to contend with heather, gorse and pine; eccentric revisions were implemented by Tom Simpson in the 1930s, but many of his arrangements were altered and even, sometimes, changed back to the original. There continue to be debates over the merits of each course, with vocal supporters on either side. The courses are similar, surrounded by heather and gorse, and both have self-contained settings for the holes.

Sunningdale is the venue for major championships and has been described as 'the ideal golf club'. Great champions have stalked the fairways, from Harry Vardon to Nick Faldo. Here, in 1956, the South African Gary Player launched his brilliant career with a win in the Dunlop Championships. In 1987, Sunningdale hosted the Ryder Cup, the first inland club in England to do so. It has been a regular venue for the International Final Qualifying round for the Open Championships.

The caddies at Sunningdale have earned a reputation for golf knowledge, while the course is admired for having class and quality. The traditional ambience of the clubhouse, with its collection of historic golf paintings and lithographs, is part of the pleasure of playing at Sunningdale.

The Old Course has been in existence since 1901; seen here is the par 3 8th hole.
The New Course is preferred by many but tends to be slightly more rugged.

Pictured on the Old Course at Sunningdale is the par 4, 17th hole with the par 4, 18th hole and clubhouse surrounded by trees directly behind.

Course Specifications

Location:	Berkshire, England
Type:	Private
Established:	1900
Total Holes:	36 (18 Old and 18 New Course)
Designed by:	Many revisions, originally Willie Park Jnr
Par:	72
Length:	6,627 yards

Wentworth England

The Wentworth Golf Club opened in 1922, offering a course designed by Harry Colt. It took the name of the great house included in the large estate bought by WG Tarrant, a builder. He used the grand building as the clubhouse and, apart from preparing a golf course; he developed a housing scheme on the estate. His ambitions were overreaching, leading to bankruptcy, and in 1931, he sold the properties to the Wentworth Estates Limited. This business belonged to Sir Lindsay Parkinson and Company.

The new owners were determined to maintain a high quality establishment, and cultivated professional golf. The Wentworth Golf Club became one of the most prestigious clubs in the country. Its international stature was confirmed when it was chosen as the venue for the Ryder Cup in 1953. The golf club still regularly hosts major tournaments, and has consistently been included in the Top 100 courses by *Golf Digest*.

Arriving at Wentworth, the leafy and rhododendron-lined drive offers glimpses through the trees of the lush fairways and manicured greens. Soon you are greeted with one of the best known sights in golf, the opening hole on the legendary West Course, overlooked by the famous castellated club house.

The club ran two courses, the West Course and the East Course, both designed by Harry Colt, and the Wentworth Company developed quality housing on the rest of the estate. In 1990, a third course, the Edinburgh, was constructed. It was designed by John Jacobs working with Gary Player and Bernard Gallacher. The Wentworth also developed a 9-hole course, the Executive. For years, the club served as headquarters of the European PGA Tour. Ernie Els, who has a house on the estate, has become closely involved with the golf club and is designing alterations to the West Course.

In 2004, the club was sold to Richard Coring for £130 million, and it is now more than a golf course. It is a major luxury leisure centre. According to the British Golf Industry Association, this is the most expensive club in Europe with high membership and green fees. This may explain the reasons behind the departure of the European PGA Tour headquarters to Dubai.

A view of the 11th green on the West Course at Wentworth, which was originally designed by Harry Colt. A recent redesign of the course was carried out by resident Professional Ernie Els.

Course Specifications

Location:	Virginia Water, Surrey, England
Established:	1922
Type:	Private
Total Holes:	18 (West, East and Edinburgh courses) 9 (Executive Course)
Designed by:	West and East: Harry Colt; Edinburgh, Executive: John Jacobs
Par:	72 (West and Edinburgh) 68 (East) 27 (Executive)
Length:	7,308 yards (West) 6,201 yards (East) 7,004 yards (Edinburgh) 1092 yards (Executive)

Woodhall Spa England

The English Golf Union, whose remit is to promote and encourage the game, owns the Woodhall Spa. The golf course was opened in 1905 on land owned by Colonel S V Hotchkins, who asked Harry Vardon to design the course. Harry Colt remodelled it in 1911 but Colonel Hotchkins, it seems, was not satisfied and he did further work on the course after World War I, making adjustments throughout the 1920s and 30s.

The Hotchkins Course has been voted as the best inland course in England, and is among the world's Top 50, but it does not allow a leisurely game. It is heath land: the heather has been described as an obstacle and the bunkers alarming. Some claim the course tends to expose a player's weaknesses, but others point out that this makes it a fine place to improve a person's game.

The sandy soil means golf can be played all year round, and golfers appreciate the narrow greens, and the variety of the 18 holes. Although not a tournament venue, it has been host to top-class international and national amateur championships, and is regarded by many as a real test of golfing ability.

Renowned for its formidable bunkers and narrow fairways, it has often been stated by the golfing press and top players alike that these are 18 great holes. Seen here is a bunker on the 451 yds par 4, 13th hole on 'the thinking man's Hotchkin Course.

There is a sister course, the Bracken, designed by Donald Steel, but it has a very different feel from that of the Hotchkins. This is designed on parkland, and uses the spacious American style of large, undulating courses. Native fauna has been allowed to repopulate the area, giving the course a highly appreciated ecological emphasis. Pine, birch and broom adorn the landscape.

The course is not as tricky as the Hotchkins, which has been described as the thinking man's course, but the Bracken does offer a strong, brisk game. Both courses are set in the enchanting scenery of Lincolnshire, and golfers do appreciate playing within pleasing landscapes.

One of Britain's finest courses, the Hotchkin is built on sandy soil which allows for year round play. Seen here is the green on the 148-yd, par 3, 5th hole.

Course Specifications

Location:	Woodhall Spa, Lincolnshire, England
Established:	1905 (Hotchkins) 1995 (Bracken)
Type:	Public
Total Holes:	18 (both courses)
Designed by:	Many revisions, originally Harry Vardon (Hotchkins) Donald Steel Designers (Bracken)
Par:	71 (Hotchkins) 73 (Bracken)
Length:	6,501 yards (Hotchkins) 5,772 yards (Bracken)

Carnoustie Scotland

It is thought that the name Carnoustie probably derives from two Scandinavian nouns, 'car' meaning rock and 'noust' meaning bay. However, there are many more fanciful explanations that local inhabitants will tell visitors.

Although the game of golf has been played over the links at Carnoustie since the 1500s, the present course, designed by Alan Robertson of St Andrews, was created in 1850. It was improved and extended to 18 holes about 20 years later by the legendary Old Tom Morris, and in 1926 the Championship course was extensively redesigned by the famous architect James Braid.

Although Braid's work was seen as a great success, it was felt that the Championship course had a weak finish. James Wright, a local man, was set the task of remedying this, and just prior to the 1937 Open Championship the final 3 holes at Carnoustie were redesigned. Wright produced what is now regarded as the toughest finishing stretch in golf.

For those looking for luxury golfing, leisure and conference facilities, the Carnoustie Hotel is one of Scotland's premium destinations. It provides enviable views over the Championship golf course, the sea or the town of Dundee. This view is looking back at the hotel from the 18th green.

Being a public links, today anybody can play at Carnoustie, with the opportunity to play the Championship course also open to those who want to test their skills. Watch out for the Barry Burn which makes its way around the final 3 holes, quietly awaiting the shot that is slightly less than perfect. It was here that Frenchman Jean Van de Velde lost the chance of making history and being crowned Open Champion in 1999.

An aerial view of the Barry Burn meandering its way over Carnoustie Golf Course. The 16th takes its name from the stream and seen here is the fairway of the 18th hole during the third round of the 136th Open Championship in July 2007.

Course Specifications

Location:	Carnoustie, Angus, Tayside, Scotland
Established:	1850
Type:	Public
Total holes:	18
Designed by:	Original course: Alan Robertson. Current course: James Braid with later modifications by James Wright.
Par:	72
Length:	6,941 yards

Loch Lomond Scotland

The lairds of Clan Colquhoun, who can trace their ancestral heritage back to the 12th century, still own the beautiful Loch Lomond golf club, which sits in 660 acres of the total estate of 55,000 acres.

This magnificent course is considered to come well within the top 100 finest golf links in the world. It is set around streams and marshlands which become natural hazards of the course; Scots pines and Douglas fir trees give it a beautiful appearance, but don't be fooled, this is no stroll; it is a demanding circuit and requires skills in all the disciplines.

Rossdhu, a Georgian manor house once home to the Colquhouns, was constructed in 1773 and today acts as the clubhouse. It is an imposing and beautiful building and replaced the 15th century Rossdhu Castle that used to stand there, which was damaged by fire.

Loch Lomond golf course boasts some of the most breathtaking scenery in world golf, with the Scottish Highlands providing the perfect backdrop. For the future, a Jack Nicklaus-designed Scottish heathland-style course is planned at Loch Lomond to add to the incredible choices afforded to Loch Lomond Golf Club members.

On a wooded peninsula guarded on three sides by the bonny banks of Loch Lomond, Rossdhu looks out across the waters. The house was resurrected as the club house for the Loch Lomond Golf Course after falling into disrepair.

Course Specifications

Location:	Luss, Alexandria, Strathclyde, Scotland
Established:	1850
Total holes:	18
Designed by:	Tom Weiskopf and Jay Morrish
Par:	71
Length:	7,100 yards

Muirfield Scotland

Muirfield was the venue for the 2002 Open Championship and is seen as one of the best courses in the world, possibly the best in the British Isles! It is the home of the Honourable Company of Edinburgh Golfers (HCEG), the world's oldest golf club, and was designed way back in 1891 by Old Tom Morris. It has hosted 15 Open Championships since 1892, the Amateur Championship on numerous occasions, the Ryder, Walker and Curtis Cups too.

In its infancy the members played over the Leith links, which consisted of five holes. In 1744 the original rules of golf were drawn up by the 'Gentlemen Golfers of Leith', ready for a tournament due to be played later the next month. These important thirteen rules became the basis of the game as we know it today, and shortly afterwards the HCEG was formed.

A great view of the 18th green, which is overlooked by the beautiful Muirfield clubhouse. A place to relax and enjoy a wonderful meal after a demanding game of golf.

It was to be a further 147 years before the course at Muirfield opened in 1891, originally as a 16-hole course: the other two holes were added shortly afterwards. In 1928 the course was altered by Harry Colt and Tom Simpson. The design is unique and very different to other courses in that it was the first to be designed with two concentric rings of nine holes. The first nine holes run clockwise around the edge, whilst the last nine run anti-clockwise on the inside of the first holes.

The opportunity to play has been made slightly more possible recently, with visitors being allowed to play on certain days and ladies being allowed to play if accompanied by a gentleman. There is much respect for Muirfield and its demanding course. Jack Nicklaus, who won here in 1966, was so taken with this links that he named his Ohio golf complex Muirfield Village.

A quite spectacular view across the golf course during the 131st British Open Championship in July 2002, sees Tiger Woods in action during the third round.

Course Specifications

Location:	Muirfield, Gullane, East Lothian, Scotland
Established:	1744
Total holes:	18
Designed by:	Old Tom Morris
Par:	73
Length:	6,970 yards

Royal Dornoch Scotland

Golf has been played on this site since 1616 but reliable records start in 1877 when Old Tom Morris designed a links course. It has been the Royal Dornoch for a hundred years and the title denotes the quality standards of the club. Despite its heritage value, the Royal Dornoch has been reinvented many times.

After World War I, the course was refurbished by both John Sutherland and Donald Rose. During World War II, the Air Ministry requisitioned the club and a wartime aerodrome was established which stretched over the ladies' 18-hole course on the lower links and 4 holes of the championship course.

After the war, it was decided to extend once again towards Embo and a plot of land, belonging to the Sutherland household, was leased and later purchased.

At this time a restricted 9-hole relief course was formed, known as the Struie, which has since been developed into a full 18-hole course with such well-known holes as the 'Caddies' Well', to name but one.

The Royal Dornoch course is narrow and difficult but is always fun to play. Here we see the 163-yard par 3, 6th hole, which takes the name of Whinny Brae.

Today the Championship Course straddles the beautiful Scottish coastline, isolated and not ideal for spectators; it is considered too short for the Open, but still ranks among the top 15 courses in the world. Tom Watson, a five-time winner of the Open, claims that the most fun he ever had was on this golf course.

Golfers can test themselves here but it is a leisurely game in rugged terrain with views up the Firth. Child players are encouraged; consequently, many a Scottish golfer has formed a lifelong attachment to golf at the Royal Dornoch club.

Child players are very much encouraged here and many Scottish golfers have learned to play on this course. The 18th green and club house can be seen here, where many social activities take place.

Course Specifications

Location:	Sutherland, Scotland
Established:	1877
Type:	Private
Total Holes:	18
Designed by:	originally Old Tom Morris
Par:	72
Length:	6,577 yards

St Andrews Old Course Scotland

The Old Course at St Andrews is generally acknowledged around the world as the 'Home of Golf', and people have been playing on the Links at St Andrews since the 1400s. It wasn't just the players that were involved with the game; ball makers, caddies and of course club makers all helped to increase interest in the game, which by the 19th century had a great following in the area.

From a simple track hacked out of the bushes and heather some 600 years ago, St Andrews has become the largest golfing complex in Europe, boasting six public golf courses.

It is interesting to note that golf in Scotland was banned by King James II in 1457, due to too many young men being distracted from their archery, a far more important skill of the period. It was only when James IV came to the throne that his attitude changed and he too became a golfer.

The Old Course hasn't always had 18 holes. By 1764 it had as many as 22 – 11 out and 11 back, although the same holes were played both ways. A decision was made that the first four holes, which were also the last four holes, were positioned too close together and should become two. Thus the course became 18 holes, the standard for today's round of golf. Sadly, as the years moved on and the sport became more popular, congestion began to cause problems. Players going out were clashing with those coming in. The solution was to have two holes per green. The outward holes would have a white flag and the inward holes a red flag, creating the now famous double greens.

It's probably fair to say that every golfer's dream is to walk on St Andrews Links, where golf has been played for over 600 years and which is generally understood to be 'the home of golf'. An incredible aerial shot shows the peninsula and parts of the Old Course.

Originally named the Society of St Andrews Golfers, and composed of 22 noblemen, professors and landowners, the Royal and Ancient Golf Club was founded in 1754. Today it governs the rules of golf everywhere except the USA.

Old Tom Morris created a separate green for the first hole, and it therefore became possible to play the course in an anti-clockwise direction, rather than clockwise as is usual. Although the course had been played clockwise and anti-clockwise on alternate weeks, it was now the anti-clockwise or right-hand circuit which had become the direction to play. It's interesting to note that many of the 112 bunkers on the course are clearly designed to catch the wayward shots of golfers playing the course on the left-hand circuit.

The first Links Act, basically safeguarding public right of way, was passed by Parliament in 1894 and saw St Andrews Town Council re-acquire the Links. They had lost control of it when they went bankrupt in 1797, after which rabbit farmers challenged the golfing community to rights to the land. Fortunately, in 1821 James Cheape of Strathtyrum, a local landowner and keen golfer, bought the land and 'saved the Links for golf.'

An elevated view of the 16th hole on the Old Course at St Andrews. This is known as 'the corner of the dyke', simply because the green is literally tucked into the corner of the dyke (or wall).

The Open Championship was played on the Old Course in 2005; the first time it was hosted there was in 1873, thus making St Andrews the course to have held the Open most often. The Dunhill Cup and subsequent Dunhill Links championship have been played at St Andrews since 1985, while many other tournaments such as the Walker Cup and the Amateur Championship have also been held at the course, along with a number of other professional and amateur competitions for both men and women.

A new organisation by the name of the St Andrews Links Trust was created via another Act of Parliament after the demise of the Town Council in 1975. This allowed the Links to continue running as a public golf course, accessible for anybody. The Castle course is a recent addition to the five 18-hole courses and one 9-hole course.

A wonderful view of the famous Swilkan Bridge, on the way to the par 4 18th hole, which is also named after the designer of the course, Old Tom Morris. The Clubhouse of the Royal and Ancient Golf Club of St Andrews can be seen in the distance.

Course Specifications

Location:	St Andrews, Fife, Scotland
Established:	1754
Type:	Links Course
Total holes:	18
Designed by:	Allan Robertson, responsible for improvements in 1848
Par:	72
Length:	6,566 yards

Turnberry Ailsa Championship Course

The Turnberry Ailsa championship course has long been regarded as one of the finest golf courses in the world, coming to prominence during the famous duel between Jack Nicklaus and Tom Watson over the four days of the 1977 Open. It was then, in brilliant sunny weather, that a capacity crowd was treated to an exhilarating display of golf from two of the best golfers the world has ever known.

The first three holes of the course pose a fairly tough opening, particularly when the wind blows from the direction of Ailsa Craig, the dramatic rock 11 miles (17.6km) out to sea.

From the admirable short fourth hole to the short 11th, the course follows the shoreline. The fifth to the eighth holes are framed by dunes, and the ninth, tenth and eleventh are flanked by craggy rocks. It is a thrilling passage full of stout hitting.

The smooth fairway of the Ailsa course, looking out to the granite dome of the Ailsa Craig.

Turnberry's ninth hole is notable, with the remote tee set on a rocky promontory on the edge of the sea; the drive across the corner of the bay offers a glimpse of the site of Bruce's Castle – Robert the Bruce, King of Scotland 1306–1329. The narrow path to the tee, and the tee shot itself, are not recommended for those of a nervous disposition.

The scenic glories of the Ailsa Course are to be savoured – the granite dome of Ailsa Craig, the low form of the tip of Argyll and the peaks of Arran, highlighted by the changing patterns of light and shade. Closer at hand, the lighthouse and the ninth's lovely back tee, are other symbols of Turnberry Ailsa, with its historic echoes.

A view of the rugged Scottish coastline and lighthouse on this challenging course.

The Turnberry clubhouse, which offers stunning panoramic views of the Ailsa and Kintyre courses, Arran and the stormy Irish Sea.

Course Specifications

Location:	Turnberry, Ayrshire, Scotland
Established:	1951
Type:	Links Course
Total holes:	18
Designed by:	Mackenzie Ross (Ailsa)
Par:	69
Length:	6,976 yards

Celtic Manor Twenty Ten Wales

It was on 28 September 2001 that the Ryder Cup Committee made the historic announcement that the 38th Ryder Cup matches would be held at the Celtic Manor Resort in the autumn of 2010. This is the first time that this famous match play tournament will be held in Wales; much of the credit for the successful bid went to the Celtic Manor Resort's commitment to build a new golf course specifically to host the Ryder Cup event.

The construction phase of the project commenced in September 2004 and was completed on schedule just two years later, with the development and construction of the new course, a new clubhouse and associated infrastructure schemes. The new Ryder Cup course is now open for limited play and has 18 holes that will challenge the best golfers in the world. Much use has been made of water hazards, which are present at half of the holes, presenting the players with classic match dilemmas. The new course features nine all-new holes (the first to the fifth, 14th, 16th, 17th and 18th holes) scattered along the Usk Valley landscape, while the remaining nine holes were from the original Wentwood Hills Championship course, although they had been extensively remodelled. A tough finishing stretch culminates in a real sting in the tail at the 18th.

Welsh golfer Bradley Dredge, standing in front of the all-new Clubhouse of the Celtic Manor Twenty Ten Golf Course.

Special attention has been paid to ensuring that spectators get the best possible views, and the design company, along with the head designer Ross McMurray, in consultation with Wentwood Hills architect Robert Trent Junior, have collaborated to ensure that the course offers better viewing than at any previous Ryder Cup match.

Raphael Jacquelin of France hits a putt on the 13th hole during the final round of the Wales Open at Celtic Manor Resort, Newport, Wales, on 1 June 2008.

Course Specifications	
Location:	Celtic Manor Resort, Newport, South Wales
Established:	2007
Total holes:	18
Designed by:	European Golf Design (EGD)
Par:	71
Length:	7,493 yards

Ballybunion Eire

This venerable golf club has a long history. It began life with 12 greens, thanks to the enthusiasm of a group of wealthy local Kerry men, all keen golfers. These influential players opened their own links in 1893. Described as a rabbit warren below a village, it staggered on until 1898, when it closed down. In 1906, Lionel Hewson, one of the original founders, was asked to design a nine-hole course for a re-opening, and in 1927 the course was extended to 18 holes. Golfers enjoyed the demands of the course, and in 1932, the Ballybunion was chosen as venue for the Irish Ladies' Championships.

Tom Simpson refurbished this links course in the 30s, and in 1971 the old clubhouse was demolished to make way for a new building. Designed by Robert Jones, a second course of 18 holes, the Cashen, was installed. Tom Watson refurbished the Old Course in 1995.

Ballybunion Old Course is located on the Shannon estuary, making it a true seaside links course. The storm clouds gather over the beautifully kept green on the 385-yard par 4, 17th hole.

The Old Course is now among the Top Ten courses in the world and is recognised as the ultimate in links golf. It is a tough course, with – among other difficulties – a 464-yard par 4 at the 11th hole. This lies on a cliff above the sea, with a rugged slope tumbling down to the dunes. Winds off the Atlantic add to the rigours of the links.

Ballybunion is said to test the best, and so, of course, attracts golfers from across the globe. Many champions have taken the risk and enjoyed this unusual course. Its historic traditions and the glory of the Irish landscape add enticing extras to the pleasure of playing at Ballybunion.

The Cashen course is less demanding but this is not to say it presents an easy game. Also a links course, it, too, embraces dunes and coastline while enduring the same Atlantic winds. The course offers a good warm-up for the Old Course.

A rather bleak and lonesome view of the green at Ballybunion Old Course, on the 359-yard, par 4 10th hole. The 453-yard, par 4 11th hole stretches along the coastline directly behind it.

Course Specifications

Location:	Ballybunion, County Kerry, Eire
Established:	1893/1906
Type:	Private
Total Holes:	18 (both courses)
Designed by:	Old Course: Tom Simpson and Tom Watson, Cashen Course: Robert Jones and Tom Watson
Par:	71 (Old) 72 (Cashen)
Length:	6,542 yards (Old) 6,477 yards (Cashen)

Royal County Down Northern Ireland

Royal County Down has hosted many wonderful championships, with the great players from the past such as Vardon, Taylor, Ball and Kirkcaldy associating themselves with the club, apparently playing 'for a purse of sovereigns'.

The great players of today still like to play there, even if not in a championship game.

Newcastle had become a very popular seaside resort by the 1880s, and it was partly this that attracted some influential Belfast businessmen to found the course in 1889. It seems that old Tom Morris was persuaded to travel to the venue 'for a sum not to exceed £4', to inspect the area and advise on a second set of nine holes – nine already existed in some form or another. After two days an 18-hole course was settled on and within a few months these were being played.

Picturesque and extremely rugged, this is the Royal County Down Golf Course in all its splendour.

As the years drifted by, work was carried out by the greens staff, much of which work was instigated by the chairman of the green, George Combe. Later, other famous names would continue to advise. People such as Harry Vardun and Ben Sayers, and then after the First World War H S Colt, submitted alterations. After the Second World War minor improvements took place, but in 1989 some important changes were made to the closing holes, and in 2004 a completely new 16th hole was designed.

Today the course is laid out in two loops of nine holes, each starting and finishing at the clubhouse. The 9th probably gives both the golfer and the spectator one of the most breathtaking views in golf, which makes it also one of the most photographed views in golf.

Today the Royal County Down course is laid out in two loops of nine holes, each starting and finishing at the clubhouse, which is seen here.

Course Specifications

Location:	Newcastle, County Down, Northern Ireland
Established:	1889
Type:	Links
Total holes:	18
Designed by:	Old Tom Morris
Par:	71
Length:	7,182 yards

Royal Portrush Northern Ireland

Royal Portrush Golf Club is considered a highly testing course, with a particularly beautiful setting. The course is situated on the North Antrim Causeway coast and has spectacular views of the hills of Donegal, Isle of Islay and Southern Hebrides, with the Giants Causeway and the Skerries to the east. The name of the course derives from the ruins of the 13th century Dunluce Castle, which overlooks the course.

It has been rated fourth in the 100 greatest courses in the British Isles by *Golf World*, ranked number 12 in the world in *Golf Magazine's* biennial rankings of the Top 100 Courses in the World, and *Golf Digest* also ranks it the third best course outside the United States.

'Beautiful but testing' is how many would describe Royal Portrush golf course. Seen here is the 6th hole on this course that ranks highly in the list of great courses of the world.

Originally founded as the 'County Club', it became 'The Royal County Club' in 1892 and assumed its present name in 1895 under the patronage of the Prince of Wales.

Fred Daly, a club member, became the first Irishman to win The Open Championship here in 1947. More recently, the course has hosted the Senior British Open Championship from 1995–99 and 2004.

Calamity Corner, the famous 14th hole, is a par 3 in excess of 200 yards; it requires a full carry to the green over an imposing ravine and is one of the highlights of the course.

Calamity Corner, the 14th and most famous hole on the Dunluce links, is one of the highlights of this enjoyable course.

Course Specifications	
Location:	County Antrim, Northern Ireland
Established:	1888
Type:	Links
Total holes:	18
Designed by:	H S Colt (Redesign 1947)
Par:	72
Length:	6,845 yards

Emirates United Arab Emirates

Dubai has successfully carved out an important role in the international golf world, helped greatly by the Emirates Golf Club. When launched in 1988, its Majlis course was described as 'The Desert Miracle', the first all-grass course in the Middle East. Here, the desert sand was tamed and adorned with lakes, while the clubhouse was designed in imitation of a grand Bedouin tent.

The Majlis underwent a refurbishment by Nick Faldo in 2006 and now has an inspired course that includes seven man-made lakes. Golfers face a true test of their skills at the challenging par 4, dog-leg eighth. Here, a straight and very confident shot is required to cover an uphill slant of 434 yards to reach a small undulating green. The eighteenth hole, too, presents a 90-degree dog-leg for the player to overcome. But there are breathtaking views and improbable lakes to compensate – it is no surprise, then, that competitors voted the Majlis the best course on the European PGA tour.

Built to imitate a Bedouin tent, the spectacular clubhouse and putting green at the Emirates golf course is shown during the second round of the Dubai Desert Classic in 2006.

The Dubai Desert Classic, played at Majlis, is an important tournament in the European PGA Tour, and this course wass also the venue for the Ladies' PGA. In December 2008 it was the scene of a sad but grand farewell by the Ladies' European Tour. The great champion Annika Sörenstam played her last tournament at Majlis before she retired from competitive golf.

The Emirates Golf Club has a second course, the Wadi, meaning 'the Valley'. Opened in 1996, this course has some daunting bunkers but is not as intimidating as the Mujlis, although equally beautiful and startling in its desert setting. The European PGA Tour plans to make Dubai its home, and Tiger Woods will be designing his first course for the deserts of Dubai.

A spectacular aerial view of the Dubai Golf Course near the Persian Gulf. The course requires an enormous amount of water for its upkeep in such high temperatures.

Course Specifications

Location:	Dubai, United Arab Emirates
Established:	1988
Type:	Private
Total Holes:	18
Designed by:	Jeremy Pern/Karl Litten
Par:	72
Length:	7,211 yards

Kingston Heath Australia

This prestigious course started life as the Elsternwick Golf Club in 1912, but a decade later the club moved to Cheltenham to become the Kingston Heath. This was not achieved without controversy; some members were so enraged that they resigned. The disruption caused by the change continued between 1923 and 1925.

The course was designed by Dan Soutar, who had been responsible for the Elsternwick course, and Dr Alister MacKenzie, but no sooner was it finished than Australia was afflicted by drought. The fairways were badly affected by dryness and cape weed. Members were so concerned that they arranged themselves into work gangs to weed the greens every weekend. The fairways recovered, of course, and Kingston Heath is now recognised as a superb, and notoriously difficult, challenge.

Seen from an elevated position are Aaron Baddeley and Greg Turner during the 2000 Holden Australian Open Golf tournament at Kingston Heath.

Golfers must assume a mood of strategic play, planning their shots with accuracy and care. The course shows a clever use of dips and hollows, and one player has claimed it has 'the best natural bunkering one would ever wish to encounter.' Although it is highly rated, some golfers believe that if only the surrounding landscape was more attractive, Kingston Heath would be the top course in Australia. It is still among the Top 100 in the world.

In 1938, the Australian Golf Union gave their approval for Kingston Heath to hold national Open and amateur championships, and the club has played a significant role in promoting golf as a popular sport in Australia. In 2003, the club won a three-year contract as the Australasian venue for the International Qualifying for the Open. In 2008, the club hosted the Australian Women's Open.

Television cameras and spectators watch avidly and quietly as Nick Faldo putts during the 2000 Holden Australian Open Golf tournament.

Course Specifications

Location:	Heatherton, Melbourne, Australia
Established:	1925
Type:	Private
Total Holes:	18
Designed by:	Dan Soutar & Dr Alister MacKenzie
Par:	72
Length:	6,947 yards

New South Wales Australia

This course has a marvellous setting on the edge of the Pacific Ocean, and was fortunate in its architects who preferred to 'let the landscape dictate the holes and create the excitement'. Thanks to these men, the course retains the wild, natural atmosphere of historic Botany Bay, where it is sited. Alister MacKenzie was the first designer and his course opened in 1928. Eric Appleby re-vamped it once in 1932 and again in 1951.

The designs have never won universal approval and have been tweaked frequently, especially during the 1980s. The weather creates continual problems, especially the strong ocean winds. Designing bunkers to withstand the winds has proved a difficult task, but modern course design and technology has managed to modify the destructive power of these forces, and the links are carefully maintained to a high standard.

Many players welcome the demands presented by the landscape, the sturdy native vegetation and the ferocious weather. Here, at the New South Wales course, enthusiasts believe they encounter the spirit of golf as it originated in the hardy climes of Scotland, and the site is spectacular. From all but five of the holes, players can see the Pacific Ocean, and if they dared wrest their concentration from the 90-foot drop at the 5th, they might catch a glimpse of whales playing in the waves.

Member players are exhilarated by the constantly changing conditions, although visitors, including the champions among them, find this course daunting. One famous member, Greg Norman, loves the challenges and the sense of adventure that every game brings.

The club hosted the Australian PGA for four years. The clubhouse is of vernacular architecture, with a low roof, a long gable and deep verandas. Its interior is elegant and classically furnished, promising comfort and quality.

From all but five of the holes, players can see the Pacific Ocean, and if they dared to wrest their concentration from the 90 foot drop at the 5th, or the snakes they could encounter, they might catch a glimpse of whales playing in the waves of the ocean.

A beautiful view of the green on the 360-metre par 4, 10th hole, with the 18th and clubhouse, which boasts spectacular views over the course to the ocean, is seen directly behind.

Course Specifications

Location:	La Perouse, New South Wales, Australia
Established:	1928
Type:	Private
Total Holes:	18
Designed by:	Alister MacKenzie and Eric Appleby
Par:	72
Length:	6,810 yards

Royal Melbourne Australia

Royal Melbourne has two current courses, known as the "East" and "West" courses. The club is seen as Australia's most prestigious, exclusive, oldest and most celebrated golf club.

Originally founded by Scottish immigrants as the Melbourne Golf Club back in 1891, it acquired its royal status from Queen Victoria in 1895. A suitable area was found near the Caulfield Railway Station for the original 18-hole course, and Tom Finlay went to work laying out the 4,750-yard course. Just six months later it was open for play.

Initially, the club location was much nearer to the city, but due to the encroaching urbanisation of the area, had to relocate. The club established itself at Black Rock, and the West Course was completed and ready for play in 1931, following a great deal of forest demolition. The East Course was completed just a year later. Over the following years there is no doubt that head greenkeeper Mick Morcom and his successor Claude Crockford made major contributions to the excellence of the two courses.

The Composite Course goes back to 1959, when Royal Melbourne was asked to hold the Canada Cup (now the World Cup). It was decided to use 12 holes from the West Course and 6 holes from the East Course, to keep the new Composite Course within the confines of the home paddock. Seen here is the green on the 135-metre par 3 7th hole on the West Course, which plays as the 7th hole on the tournament Composite Course.

In 1959 the club was invited to hold the Canada Cup – today known as the World Cup – with some 20,000 spectators expected. The decision was made to hold the tournament on what is known as the "composite course". This was made up by using 12 West Course holes and 6 East Course holes. Used many times since, its success is beyond a doubt, having been regularly rated in the top ten best courses in the world.

In 1991 the club celebrated its Centenary with memorable events and activities that paid tribute to both its age and the pleasure that the club gives.

This is the sprawling new clubhouse at Royal Melbourne Golf Club. At 3pm on Tuesday 12 October 1982, the old clubhouse was destroyed by fire. This was almost 50 years to the day after the clubhouse that was built in 1905 was also burnt to the ground.

Course Specifications

Location:	Black Rock, Victoria, Australia
Established:	1891
Type:	Links
Total holes:	18
Designed by:	Alex Russell / Dr Alister MacKenzie
Par:	72
Length:	7,002 yards

Cape Kidnappers New Zealand

Cape Kidnappers is a spectacular course, set on fingers of land spreading into the ocean of Hawke's Bay. Once a vast sheep farm, the course was designed by Tom Doak, who said, 'The site is not like anywhere else in golf'. It is certainly a challenging course, its terrain without sand dunes but with jutting cliffs that tilt towards the sea.

Cliff-top holes and high winds test the skills of the most resilient golfer. The green is barely 22 yards long. The sixth hole is a par 3 across a deep gully and the fifteenth, known as Pirate's Plank, is favoured by high winds and set close to a colony of gannets. There are moments when the ball is in danger of being knocked into the sea. As can be imagined, golfers at the nineteenth hole swap epic tales of games played at Cape Kidnappers.

Captain James Cook named the place during his explorations of the Pacific Ocean in the 18th century. The clubhouse is designed to honour a traditional sheep-shearing shed, and the club prides itself on having a course that has 'interesting holes you wouldn't find anywhere else', to quote the architect. Certainly, it has quickly gained the reputation of a course that tests even the best of golfers, and despite its newness has been voted among the 50 best courses in the world.

Players develop a fierce, determined spirit when faced with the proximity of the ocean to the rugged cliff course and the challenge of beating the pervading wind. The beauty of the country and the unusual design of the Kidnappers Bay course attract all eager sportsmen. Copious notes and advice are offered to hopefuls so that they may be prepared for the terrain, which recalls old-time Scottish courses.

Cape Kidnappers is not a classic links course, with its wrinkles of sand dunes. The land tilts toward the sea as a series of ridges jutting out towards the edge of the cliffs. Yet the play is seaside golf at its finest, as can be seen here at the green of the 403-yard, par 4, 9th hole, with the 5th a little way in the distance.

A spectacular aerial view showing the 15th, 16th and 17th holes at Cape Kidnappers golf course on the rugged coast at Hawkes Bay in New Zealand.

Course Specifications

Location:	Te Awanga, Hawke's Bay, North Island, New Zealand
Established:	2004
Type:	Private
Total Holes:	18
Designed by:	Tom Doak
Par:	72
Length:	7,137 yards

Durban Country Club South Africa

South Africa's oldest club, the Royal Durban, hosted the 1919 National Golf Championship, and it was after this that the decision was made to build a new club. The Royal Durban course became so waterlogged during the championship that the winner took an incredible 320 very watery strokes to finish. After this debacle, and the thought of further floods, pressure mounted for a new course to be constructed.

The following year a plot of land was secured and George Waterman and Laurie Waters, four times winners of the South African Open, were given the task of designing the new course. On 9 December 1922 the all-new course was ceremonially opened, and within two years the Durban Country Club, as it became known, hosted the first of many South African Open Tournaments. Since then many of the great players have golfed here, and here in 1956 Gary Player conquered his first South African Open. With further regular wins in the interim years, he returned in 1969 to score a 273, including a record round of 64.

The course overlooks the beautiful Blue Lagoon estuary and the Indian Ocean, while the classic Cape Dutch-style clubhouse stands prominently over the course, giving it elegance and a sense of timelessness.

David Howell of England chips onto the first green during the first round of the South African Airways Open, at Durban Country Club, on 20 January 2005.

An elevated, general view of the first green during the first round of the South African Airways Open at Durban Country Club on 20 January 2005.

Course Specifications

Location:	Durban, KwaZulu Natal, South Africa.
Established:	1922
Type:	Semi-links golf course
Total holes:	18
Designed by:	George Waterman and Laurie Waters
Par:	72
Length:	6,683 yards

Hirono Japan

Charles Alison, responsible for designing many of Japan's greatest golf courses, also put his hand to the stunning layout that today is the Hirono golf course. It is thought that its outstanding beauty may well have been inspired by Alison's visit to the magnificent gardens in Kyoto.

Credit must be given to Chozo Ito for turning Alison's plans into reality. Recently returned from a tour of the world's greatest golf courses, he used the photographs he had taken of bunkers, greens and other features as reference. Seiichi Takahata, who was overseeing the project, often found himself at odds with Ito, but without doubt, whoever made the final decision, the results were spectacular. Hirono opened on 19 June 1932 and today it is a prestigious private club situated just outside the city of Kobe.

Hirono is not only a beautiful course but it challenges the player to his or her limits. It has hosted most of Japan's biggest championship games and is well known for its final three very different holes, which have seen many a potential champion slip up at the last section of the course. During an exhibition match in 1963, Jack Nicklaus became the first man to reach the 565-yard, par 5 15th hole in two shots – an achievement to which few can aspire.

The beautiful 167-yard, par 3, 13th hole, on the Hirono Golf Club course. This was the venue for the 2005 Japan Open.

The rolling parkland style layout of the Hirono course features many tree-lined fairways and heavily-bunkered green complexes. Seen here is the 351-yard, par 4, 10th hole.

It is difficult to get a game at this wonderful club, but if you do, take a stroll over to the colonial style clubhouse and browse around the little golf museum they have there.

Course Specifications

Location:	Kobe, Japan
Established:	1932
Type:	Private
Total holes:	18
Designed by:	Charles Alison
Par:	72
Length:	6,925 yards

Valderrama Spain

This splendid course is consistently rated as having the best fairways in Europe. It was designed in 1974 by Robert Trent Jones Snr, when the course was known as Sotogrande New. In 1971, it was named Las Aves and then, in 1984, the name finally became Valderrama, taking the title of the old aristocratic estate on which the club was built.

Robert Trent Jones Snr reworked the course in 1984, and walked it many times before making any design decisions. His aim was to make something that demanded the golfer employ precision thinking and play a methodical game. But he wanted, also, for Valderrama to appeal to the Sunday golfer as well as to first-class players. His care and attention paid off. The year after Valderrama hosted the 1988 Volvo Masters, the flagship tournament of the European PGA Tour, his course was recognized as the best in the European rankings and it has held this position ever since.

In 1997, Valderrama was chosen as the venue for the Ryder Cup, the first time a European course was selected for this prestigious championship. Seve Ballesteros, then captain of the European team, declared, 'I found everything perfect. It is impossible to imagine a golf course in a better condition.' Other prestigious tournaments selected Valderrama as their venue. It hosted the World Golf Championships in 1999, when the winner was Tiger Woods, and in 2000 the American Express tournament was played here. Mike Weir was the champion.

The connection between Volvo and Valderrama was celebrated in 2008, the 20th anniversary since the first Volvo Masters. The full programme has not been unfolded, but the tournament will be celebrated with various festivities. The clubhouse is an impressive building in the Spanish hacienda style, and houses dining and recreational facilities of the highest quality.

A view of the par 4, 5th hole, 'Los Altos', which can be seen in the distance at the Valderrama Golf Club in Southern Spain. The tee is raised and gives splendid views over the rolling countryside.

The course is located in Andalucia, the largest and southernmost region of Spain, and the climate is ideal for year-round golf. This is a view of the par 4 finishing hole at Valderrama.

Course Specifications

Location:	Andalucia, Spain
Established:	1974
Type:	private
Total Holes:	18
Designed by:	Robert Trent Jones Snr
Par:	71
Length:	7,148 yards

Most golfers will have their favourite golfer, their hero, whom they either follow, try to emulate or just admire. There have been some great players over the years, and recently we have been privileged to see one of the greatest ever – Tiger Woods. He has already broken records, achieved things no other golfer has, and most of all he will without doubt continue to astound and entertain.

In the Hall of Fame, we have tried to choose golfers who have played significant roles over the years, who have contributed something to the world of golf and who have reached the pinnacle of greatness within their sport.

Deep down they are just like you and me, but they have a gift, a skill of which they have taken full advantage – they can play a great game of golf.

Today these great players can earn huge wages and, like other major sportsmen, they have become involved with large sponsors who pump millions of dollars into the game. These golfers are well-known celebrities, and they have to be at the top of their game or they can so easily end up in that large bunker of has-beens.

Bobby Locke

Phil Mickelson

Seve Ballesteros

Lee Trevino

Jack Nicklaus

Bobby Jones

Walter Hagen

Ben Hogan

Gary Player

Tom Watson

Sam Snead

Gene Sarazen

Arnold Palmer

Nick Faldo

Annika Sörenstam

Tiger Woods

Bobby Locke (1917 – 1987)

Bobby Locke was an eccentric personality and his quirky ways did not endear him to all his competitors. His clothes were distinctive for he invariably appeared in linen dress shirts with neck-ties, flannel plus-fours and white buckskin shoes. It was rumoured that he would murmur to the ball before whacking it. Bobby was infamous for moving very slowly during the game, while ignoring the annoyance of other players or threats from officials. His placid expression and unflappable style earned him the nickname 'Muffin Face'.

Bobby was a South African, born in Germiston on 20 November 1917. He taught himself to play golf, following the instructions in books written by Bobby Jones. Although his game lacked grace, he is often described as the greatest putter in history. He won numerous junior, provincial and state amateur championships in his native South Africa. When he turned professional in 1938, he won the South African, New Zealand and Irish Opens.

Bobby went on to the USA, where in just over three years he played in 59 tournaments, winning 11, coming second in 10 and reaching the top four 13 times. Despite his penchant for partying and his placid manners, Bobby aroused hostility in the USA, and after winning the British Open in 1949, chose to play mainly in Britain. Defying PGA rules, he played in unofficial events in the US, and this barred him from the PGA Tour. This ban was later lifted and he dominated the PGA Tour, winning four Open Championships within eight years. He won tournaments in Australia, France, Egypt and South Africa, and in 1957 he won three Open Championships in a row.

In 1959, Bobby was badly injured in a car accident, forcing him to retire from professional golf. In 1987, almost 30 years later, he died in Johannesburg, South Africa.

South African Bobby Locke playing a shot in the 1951 Daks tournament at Sunningdale.

Bobby Locke was known for his extreme preparation prior to a shot. He always took great care and time before committing himself.

Phil Mickelson (1970 –)

Philip Mickelson was born in San Diego, California on 16 June 1970, and later the family moved to Arizona. His parents taught him to play golf, and in copying his father, the boy learned to play left-handed. Inevitably, once he joined the professional circuit, Phil was nicknamed 'Lefty'.

His parents were cautious about allowing the young Phil to enter competitions; nevertheless, as a junior golfer, he won 34 San Diego junior titles. At Arizona State University, Phil's golfing achievements were spectacular. Tall and with an athletic build, during his four years of study he won the NCAA championships three times, was only the second student to earn the first-team All-American honour and in 1990 was the first left-handed player to win the US Amateur championship.

Phil graduated as a Psychology Major in 1992, but in 1994 he chose to become a professional golfer. His game is consistently of a high standard and Phil became known as 'the best golfer in the world without a major victory'. He broke this pattern in 2004 with a major win at the US Masters and another at the 2005 US PGA Championship. Phil attained his greatest moment when he won the 2006 Masters, playing against Tiger Woods. In May 2008, he emerged as victor in the Crown Plaza Invitational.

His career is on an upward trajectory, and his form improves year on year, but he faces fierce competition in Tiger Woods, Vijay Singh and a new generation of players. Phil is attached to the Grayhawk Golf Club in Scottsdale, Arizona. He lives in Rancho Santa Fe, California with his wife Amy, whom he courted at Arizona State University and married in 1991. They have three children.

Ponte Vedra Beach, Florida, USA. Phil Mickelson chips onto the 16th green during the second round of The Players Championship on The Players' Stadium Course at the Tournament Players' Club, Sawgrass on 9 May 2008.

Phil Mickelson with the winner's trophy during the fourth and final round of the Crowne Plaza Invitational at Colonial Country Club on 25 May 2008 in Fort Worth, Texas, USA.

Seve Ballesteros (1957 –)

Severiano Ballesteros grew up surrounded by golfers. His uncle was a professional golfer and his brothers were keen players. This may account for Seve's enthusiastic participation in team matches, proved by his adult Ryder Cup record.

Seve was born in Pedrena, Spain on 9 April 1957 and, as a boy, used to play golf with his family on the beach. Seve was only 16 when he became a professional, and astounded the golfing world when he tied second with Jack Nicklaus in the 1974 British Open. He won the Spanish National Championship for Under 25s and again in 1975. Victory in many international tournaments led him to his first major championship win when he won the British Open in 1979 and the Masters in 1980. Between 1980 and 1988, Seve won three major tournaments.

He played for the European Ryder Cup team nine times, and was part of a winning team five times, the last occasion being in 1997 when he was the non-playing captain. He was on the winning teams at the World Cup of Golf, The Seve Trophy and The Royal Trophy.

Seve is continental Europe's most successful player, and in 2000 the Golf Digest magazine ranked him the sixteenth greatest player in history after he had been inducted into the World Golf Hall of Fame in 1999. By the early '90s, Seve had won 5 major championships, 9 PGA Tours, 49 European Tours, and 36 other international games, but his career was blighted by back problems, forcing him into retirement in 2007.

Seve has a successful course design company and has been selected as the non-playing captain to the 2008 European team in the Royal Trophy against the Asian team. His home is in Santander, Spain but he is divorced from Carmen, whom he married in 1988. They have three children.

Ballesteros was admitted to hospital in Madrid on 6 October 2008, after fainting at Madrid's international airport before boarding a flight to Germany.

He battled through four separate major operations, which included a 6-hour procedure to remove a brain tumour. It was reported by the hospital in November 2008 that he was starting his rehabilitation in the intensive care unit. Ballesteros was released from hospital shortly afterwards and continued to be treated and monitored by the hospital.

Spanish golfer Seve Ballesteros during the US Masters golf tournament held at Augusta, USA during April 1988.

Severiano Ballesteros holds the trophy aloft after winning the final round of the Sun Alliance PGA Championship at the Royal St George's golf course in Sandwich, Kent, UK, on 30 May 1983. Ballesteros won the championship with a 4-round total of 287, shooting a final round of 71.

Lee Trevino (1939 –)

Lee Buck Trevino was born in Dallas, Texas on 1 December 1939. He never knew his father, but his grandfather Trevino helped bring him up. When Lee was a small child, his uncle gave him some old golf equipment. Thereafter, he played golf endlessly, and as an eight-year-old became a caddy.

He joined the Marine Corps when he was 17, and after his discharge he became a club professional in El Paso, gambling for stakes in head-to-head matches. In 1967, he joined the PGA Tour, coming fifth behind Jack Nicklaus and earning six thousand dollars. Lee was named Rookie of The Year by *Golf Digest* magazine, and he presented a serious rival to Jack.

Lee won the 1971 US Open, beating Jack, and then the Canadian Open and the Open Championships. His record for these three wins in one year was not matched until 20 years later by Tiger Woods. *Sports Illustrated* named him their Sportsman of The Year and *Wide World of Sports* chose him as Athlete of The Year. By the end of 1972, he had 10 wins under his belt. In 1974 he was in fine form, winning the PGA Open Championship, but then in 1975 Lee was struck by lightning.

After surgery for severe spinal injuries, Lee returned, retaining his customary wit and cheerful manners. Although no longer a consistent winner in major tournaments, he remained an important player. In 1980, he was ranked second in McCormack's World Golf Rankings and during the '80s, he was second to Jack Nicklaus in the PGA career money list.

Lee has proved very successful in the Senior PGA Tour, where he has achieved 29 wins. His rough golf style is exciting, while his humour and easy manners have helped make the Senior Tour popular (it is now called the Champions Tour). He appears in movies and has been spoofed on *The Simpsons*.

14 July 1980: Lee Trevino of the USA, joint leader during the Open at Muirfield.

10 August 1974, PGA Championship. Lee Trevino in action from the bunker at Tanglewood Championship Course, Winston Salem, North Carolina, USA.

Jack Nicklaus (1940 –)

He has been called 'the perfect ambassador for golf', a description that acknowledges the qualities of courtesy and sportsmanship for which he is renowned.

Jack Nicklaus was born on 21 January 1940 in Columbus, Ohio. His career began as his father's caddy but, inspired by Bobby Jones' example, Jack won the US Amateurs in 1959. He went on to achieve 113 victories around the world, including the Masters in 1986 when he was 46 years old, and 8 Senior PGA tours.

Jack enrolled in Ohio State University. However, golf was his passion and this made him not only a champion player but also led him into designing golf clubs and courses, and to making films and books teaching the game. He built a sporting empire, under the brand 'The Golden Bear' – a nickname given to Jack himself. Between 1964 and 1976 he was Top Money Winner eight times on the professional circuit and, in 1993, was named Golf Course Architect of the World by *Golf World Publications*.

Jack has had 73 PGA tours, and has won six Masters, five PGA championships, four US Opens, three British Opens and two US Amateurs. *GOLF* magazine, in their work 'Centennial of Golf in America 1888–1988', named Jack as Golfer of the Century. Ohio State University is home to the Jack Nicklaus Museum, where memorabilia of his life and awards can be viewed.

In his private life, Jack has found happiness with his wife, Barbara, their five children and 21 grandchildren. The National Golf Foundation named them as Golf Family of the Year in 1985; in 1992, The Metropolitan Golf Writers Association awarded the Nicklaus clan Family of the Year, and in 1999, Jack was honoured as Father of the Year by the Minority Golf Association of America.

But the great champion credits his luck to the three pennies and a buckeye (a horse chestnut, the mascot of Ohio State) that he carries in his pocket whenever he plays a game of golf!

The concerned look on the face of the young Jack Nicklaus is clear. From an early age he was known for his power of concentration, which ultimately rewarded him with unparalleled success.

Baltusroll Golf Club, Springfield, New Jersey, 1980. Jack Nicklaus, seen on the lower course celebrating after another successful putt.

Bobby Jones (1902 – 1971)

Bobby Jones had 'the temper of a timber wolf', but he was a brave, creative man and a stylish golfer.

He was born a sickly child on 17 March 1902 in Atlanta, Georgia, yet he quickly showed talent as a golfer and, at 14 years of age, won the East Lake Invitational and the Georgia Amateur championships. He was the youngest ever to play in the US Amateur Championships.

During 1922–23, Bobby travelled with American golfers to Britain, but his game at the British Open and at St Andrews was well below standard. Incidentally, this tour was to develop into the Walker Cup.

In 1923 Bobby won the US Open, and over the next seven years won at least one championship every year, winning 62 per cent of all the national championships he entered. When he won both the US and British Open, he was given a tickertape parade down Broadway. In 1930 he won the US Amateur, US Open, British Amateur and British Open, the first player to win all four championships in one calendar year. This achievement was the first to be described as a 'Grand Slam'.

Then Bobby Jones, at 28 years old, retired. But he did not leave golf. He designed the first matched, mass-produced set of clubs. Made of steel, each was identified by a number, replacing the long-used Scottish names, and these designs remained in use for 40 years. In 1931, he made 12 classic films, 'How I Play Golf', but his enduring legacy is the Atlanta National course, now home to the Masters. He designed and opened it in 1933.

He joined the US Army in 1940, but in 1948 Bobby was diagnosed with a rare degenerative disease of the central nervous system, syringomyelia. He showed great courage despite having to depend on a wheelchair to move about. At his death on 18 December 1971, his obituaries lamented the loss of 'the greatest of them all'.

R W Hartley (left) walks with the American golfer Bobby Jones to the next green during the 1930 Walker Cup contest (Britain v USA) at Royal St George's Links at Sandwich, UK.

20 June 1930. American Bobby Jones takes a swing during the Open Championship at Hoylake, which he went on to win.

Walter Hagen (1892 – 1969)

Walter Hagen was, it is claimed, the first millionaire golf player. He was a colourful character, swanning around in a chauffeur-driven limousine and hosting an endless round of parties. A dandy, he was listed among America's best-dressed men.

Walter was born in Rochester, New York in 1892 and revealed an early skill at baseball. However, he preferred golf and worked as a caddy when he was a mere 12 years old. When he was 17, he became a professional golfer. During his career he had 44 Tour victories and won 11 Major Championships playing in the US Open, the British Open and the PGA Championship. He was captain of each of the first six US Ryder Cup teams. Only Jack Nicklaus and Tiger Woods have bettered his 11 major wins.

It was his determination to bring status to golfers and all professional sportsmen that has ensured his place in the Hall of Fame. His style was flamboyant and showy, and this attracted a huge popular following. It is said that he was the first golfer to capitalise on product endorsements, and further increased his tournament income by charging fees for exhibition matches.

But making money was not his first concern; Walter said, 'I never wanted to be a millionaire. I just wanted to live like one'. He was motivated by a love of the game and it is due to his efforts that the PGA came to be accepted as a respectable, important sporting body. He travelled widely, persuading clubs in the US and many other countries to employ and use professionals. His efforts on behalf of professional golfers made it possible for players in the early twentieth century to earn a decent living or even become very rich.

Maddening, unpunctual and charming, Walter also had 'unmatched putting abilities'. He was sadly missed when he died on 6 October 1969.

American golfer Walter Hagen hands back the Ryder Cup trophy (held by the USA team) to Mr J Batley, of the Professional Golfers Association, after their arrival in England in April 1929, for the upcoming Ryder Cup tournament.

Walter Hagen on the fairway at a local course at Cleveland, Ohio, USA, during a round of golf in July 1925.

Ben Hogan (1912 – 97)

His cold, haughty expression and pale blue eyes earned Ben Hogan the title of 'The Hawk' in the US, while in Scotland he was 'The Wee Ice Man'. He was a careful, methodical player but he was also a determined, courageous man, winning many fans despite his aloof style.

Ben Hogan was born on 12 August 1912 in Stephenville, Texas. Biographers explain that Ben's introverted personality stemmed from the trauma of witnessing his father's suicide when he was nine years old, yet no one is sure Ben was a witness. After his father's death, Ben supplemented the family income by working as a caddy and turned professional golfer when he was 17.

His first ten professional years were not promising. Then, in 1940, he won three consecutive tournaments, and between then and 1959 he totalled 63 professional tournament wins. Not that Ben golfed throughout this decade. War service interrupted, and in 1949, Ben was injured in a motor accident. He was told he would never walk again but in 1953 Ben, albeit with bandaged legs, went on to win the Masters, the US Open and the British Open, the first player to win three major tournaments in one year. The record stood until 2001 when Tiger Woods achieved the same.

Ben would not play in the PGA Championship, mainly because his injured legs could not manage the 36-hole event. But when he retired in 1971, he had 64 wins on the PGA Tour, nine major championships and had been named three times as PGA Player of The Year. His major wins were equalled by Gary Player, and beaten only by Jack Nicklaus, Tiger Woods and Walter Hagen.

Ben's book, *Five Lessons: The Modern Fundamentals of Golf*, is currently in its 64th reprint. He married Valerie Fox in 1935, and they lived in Fort Worth, Texas. He died there on 25 July 1997, mourned as a champion among champions. Golf nerds continue to argue that Ben was actually a left-handed person playing right-handed golf!

A portrait of Ben Hogan (1912 – 1997) taken around 1955, leaning on a golf club at a green in the USA.

A great early colour picture of Ben Hogan taking a swing during a game of golf sometime in June 1955.

Gary Player (1936 –)

'The Black Knight', Gary Player, is not only one of the world's great golfers, but is respected for using his huge sporting fortune to promote education in the developing world, and for his tireless efforts to popularise the game of golf. In 2000 he was given the PGA Tour Ambassador of Golf Award.

Gary Player always dressed in black on the course, whence came his nickname. Born in 1936 in Johannesburg, South Africa, he became a professional when he was 17 years old. Three years later, he joined the PGA Tour and, in 1985, the Champions Tour. He went on to compete in 24 US PGA Tours, won three Masters, three British Opens, two PGA Championships and the US Open. Then, as a veteran, he won nine Senior Players' Championships.

His other victories make a very long list, and his impressive achievements were recognized when he was inducted into the World Golf Hall of Fame in 1974. Also, he was named South African Sportsman of the Century and the NEC World Championship of Golf Trophy was named 'The Gary Player Cup'.

Gary is one of five players to make the Grand Slam and is the last player to have won three tournaments in a row on the PGA Tour. He is the only champion who has won the British Open in three different decades. Honorary degrees, including Doctor of Laws from St Andrews, Scotland and Doctor of Science from the University of Ulster, Northern Ireland, have been conferred on him. He was presented with the Hilton Hotel Lifetime Achievement Award in 1995. In 2003, he received the Laureus Lifetime Achievement Award at the Laureus World Sports Awards. Shell Oil appointed Gary 'Global Ambassador to Shell's Wonderful World of Golf'.

Gary is a highly respected racehorse breeder, as well as a course and golf equipment designer. He and his wife Vivienne have six children and 13 grandchildren, and today he devotes his time to his educational charities and public speaking.

Gary Player of South Africa is pictured in action during the 1984 US Masters at the Augusta National Golf Club in Augusta, Georgia, USA.

South African Gary Player lifts the claret jug after winning the 1974 British Open at Royal Lytham St Anne's Golf Club, which took place during July at Lytham, Lancashire, England.

Tom Watson (1949 –)

Tom Watson's career had a weak beginning and, for a while, he was perceived as a player who wilted under pressure. This image seemed to go with his boyish, freckled appearance and he was dubbed 'Huckleberry Dillinger'.

He was born in Kansas City, Missouri on 4 September 1949 and his father was a golfer who encouraged Tom's innate talent. Before turning professional, Tom won four Missouri State Amateur championships. His early career faltered, but under the guidance of the golfer Byron Nelson he won the Western Open in 1974. At the British Open in 1977 he beat Jack Nicklaus by one, thrilling, stroke. His other spectacular win over Jack was at the US Open in 1982 with a margin of two shots.

Tom played on five Ryder Cup teams between 1993, when he was captain, and 1997. He was named PGA Player of the Year six times, and in 1987 was given the Bob Jones Award, a very high accolade. He had the rare honour of being the Golf Professional Emeritus at the Greenbrier Resort, White Sulpher Springs. Sam Snead is the only other golfer to have held this post.

Tom reached the Top Ten in World Ranking, but he was also admired as a sound all-rounder and supportive team player. In 1991, he gained wider recognition beyond his talents as a golfer when he resigned from the Kansas City Country Club, which refused Jews membership. Only after the Club changed its exclusive policy did Tom agree to rejoin the place.

Despite a lapse in the standard of his game during the 1980s, Tom was a great champion with many wins behind him. He has made at least one PGA Tour cut every year since 1971, winning the 1998 MasterCard Colonial when he was 48 years old. He has written numerous books on the game, and in 1988 was inducted into the World Golf Hall of Fame. He lives in Kansas with his wife, two children and three stepchildren.

American golfer Tom Watson holding the trophy after winning the British Open Golf Championship, held at Royal Birkdale on 17 July 1983.

Tom Watson takes another swing on the last stretch of the game that would see him winning the British Open Golf Championship, at the Royal Birkdale Golf Club in July 1983.

Sam Snead (1912 – 2001)

As a boy, Sam Snead was a keen athlete excelling in all games, but golf was his favourite. He started working as a seven-year-old caddie and, he claimed, was so hooked on the game that his father helped Sam to carve a redwood driver to practise his game. Although in adolescence he was an All-American footballer, his coach Harold Bell told him to concentrate on golf.

Sam was the youngest of five brothers and one sister. He was born in Ashwood, Virginia, and became a professional golfer in 1934 when he left high school. He lost his first tournament, in which Gene Sarazen was competing, by one shot. In 1936 he won the Virginia Pro-Amateur, joined the PGA Tour and won his first major victory. His powerful drive quickly earned him the title 'Slammin' Sammy Snead'.

During his long career, Sam was to win first place 185 times and second place 63 times. He was in the Top Ten 358 times, and made 42 holes-in-one. His style was not elegant, but Sam shrugged off his critics. Winning was what mattered, he declared. By the end of his career, Sam had achieved 82 PGA Tour victories and 14 Senior PGA wins.

He was a member of the US Ryder Cup team ten times, and in four Canada Cup team tournaments. He won his last Masters in 1954, when he competed against Ben Hogan, and set a record when, at the age of 52, he won a PGA event. Then, at 70 years old, he won his final Senior PGA Tour victory. He was awarded the PGA Tour Lifetime Achievement Award in 1998, having been inducted into the World Golf Hall of Fame in 1974. He was also the first player to be made Golf Professional Emeritus at the Greenbrier Resort, White Sulphur Springs.

Sam married his childhood sweetheart, Audrey Kanes, in 1940, and they settled in Hot Springs, Virginia. He died in 2001.

A photograph taken around 1937 shows American golfer Sam Snead making a putt during a tournament at Nassau in the Bahamas.

A close-up shot of Sam Snead, showing him in action during The Masters in 1972, held at the Augusta National Golf Course in Augusta, Georgia, USA.

Gene Sarazen (1902 – 1999)

Gene Sarazen was only 5 foot 4 inches tall, yet he was immensely strong and athletic. His long life was devoted to golf, starting as a ten-year-old caddie and ending when he died aged 97. He was famous, too, for always wearing the knickerbockers and plus-fours on the course that were fashionable when he began his career as a youth.

On 27 February 1902, Gene was born into an Italian family in Harrison, New York. When he was 20, he won two major championships, the PGA and US Open. He became one of five Career Grand Slam golfers, and the winner of 39 PGA tournaments. He played in the US Ryder Cup team six times. And between 1922 and 1933 he won altogether seven major championships across the Masters, US Open, British Open and the PGA Tournaments.

Gene was the first prominent golfer to employ the interlocking grip, and he introduced a very effective sand-specific club, the sand wedge. Gene designed and used it to win the British Open in 1932; golfers still use the sand wedge. In the same year, he was recognized as Male Athlete of the Year by Associated Press.

In 1935, trailing behind the leader, Craig Wood, in the Masters, Gene achieved a rare albatross two on the hole, emerging as champion. The organisers had to tear up the cheque already made out to Craig!

In the 1970s, Gene appeared at top events as a player, but he extended his golfing interests. He endorsed Wilson Sporting Goods for 75 years, became commentator on the television show, *Wonderful World of Golf*, and between 1981 and 1999, he would hit a ceremonial opening tee shot before each Masters Tournament. In 1974, he was inducted into the World Golf Hall of Fame and in 1992, was voted the Bob Jones Award, the highest accolade given by the United States Golf Association.

Gene died in Florida in 1999, mourned as a great golfer who had introduced millions to the joy of the game.

American golfer Gene Sarazen with a trophy at the 1932 British Open Golf Championships at Princes' Course, Sandwich, England.

An undated picture of an older Gene Sarazen taken during *The Masters* tournament.

Arnold Palmer (1929 –)

Arnold Palmer dominated the 1950s to the 1970s, and his fame was enhanced when he co-founded The Golfing Channel series for television. His talents keep him on the list of America's richest sportsmen even at his grand age.

Arnold is the son of a greenskeeper, so golf was part of his life from the moment he was born at Latrobe, Pennsylvania on 10 September 1929. When he was a teenager, he won five West Penn Amateur Championships. After serving in the Coast Guard, he returned to golf and in 1954 won the US Amateur. He turned professional, and during the PGA Tours of 1957 he won four times; in 1958 he won the Masters. In both 1960 and 1962, Arnold was champion eight times in matches that included the Masters and the US Open. He was the first four-time winner of the Masters and played the final one of his 62 wins on the PGA Tour in 1971.

Following the example of previous champions, Arnold developed a business empire around golf equipment, courses, clothing lines and similar sports products. He returned to the game when he joined the Senior PGA Tour in 1980. His glamour and bold golfing style have ensured that his popularity with spectators and television viewers has never waned. His fans are known as 'Arnie's Army' because in 1958, during the Masters Tournament, troops from a local army base turned up to support the swashbuckling golfer. Thereafter, his legions of fans were identified with the enthusiastic soldiers.

Arnold is a Career Grand Slam Player who has won many championships and has been awarded many honours. His nickname, 'The King', reveals his high standing. Arnold, a skilled pilot, has bought his own aircraft, but he spends much of his fortune on medical research and charities, particularly those for women and children.

Arnold Palmer is shown taking a golf swing during an unidentified tournament, as spectators watch on the sidelines.

A young Arnold Palmer, photographed around 1953. Little did he know that one day he would be regarded by many as one of the greatest players in the history of men's professional golf.

Nick Faldo (1959 –)

Nick Faldo found success through determination rather than innate brilliance. He was born in 1957 in Welwyn Garden City, England and showed no interest in golf until he was 14 years old, when he watched Jack Nicklaus on television. Four years later, Nick won the English Amateur and the British Youths Championships. He was also the youngest-ever player chosen for the Ryder Cup.

Nick did not show form in the early 1980s, giving poor performances at the 1983 British Open and the 1984 Masters. He withdrew, to be coached by David Leadbetter, and in 1987 won the British Open by one shot. Steady under pressure, some of his victories were very close, but between 1987 and 1996 he won more in the four major tournaments than any other player. He won the British Open in 1990 and 1992, and The Masters in 1989 and 1990. In 1992, he was top of the Official World Golf Ranking for 98 weeks and his earnings broke world records.

Nick's record on the Ryder Cup has not been surpassed. He won the highest number of points (25) during the 11 tours in which he represented the Europeans. Named PGA Tour Player of The Year in 1990, he won 29 European Tour titles. Nick won his final major championship at the 1996 Majors. He won 39 individual tournaments, and has won tours and played in invitational events around the world. In 1997 he was inducted into the World Golf Hall of Fame and was awarded an MBE in 1998.

Nick is a course designer and owns golf schools and shops. He set up the Faldo Series for young golfers and, with the Marriott Hotel group, established the Faldo Golf Institute for all players. Not known as a flamboyant personality, his private life has been more colourful than most. He has had three wives, and one furious girlfriend made the headlines when she wielded a golf club to batter Faldo's Porsche 959.

English golfer Nick Faldo holds the trophy after winning the Colgate PGA Championship held at Royal Birkdale, 6 August 1978.

Nick Faldo competing in the British Open at Muirfield, Scotland, July 1987. Faldo went on to win the competition.

Annika Sörenstam (1970 –)

From early childhood, Annika was a superb athlete, but as a teenager was so shy that she would deliberately lose her games to avoid making the victor's speech. She was born in Bro, Sweden, on 9 October 1970 to a family of keen sportsmen. As a girl, Annika won numerous amateur championships and attended the University of Arizona, where her game was nurtured. She was the first non-American to win the NCAA National Championship. In 1992 she was named World Amateur Champion.

Annika turned professional in 1992, having her first important win in the 1994 LPGA tour, when she was named Rookie of The Year. In 1995, she won the Australian Ladies' Masters and two tournaments in the LET. She was the first to top both the European and LPGA money lists within one year. She finished the '90s as winner of two US Women's Opens and the Du Maurier Classic, and her successes brought her Sweden's prestigious Jerringpriset award. She was the first non-American to win the Vare Trophy. And, in 1997, she found time to marry David Esch.

The decade ended with the rise of a major competitor, Karrie Webb. Annika changed her caddie, revised her exercise programme and, in 2001, had eight LPGA wins, and again was awarded the Vare Trophy. In 2002, she added to her wins, becoming the second golfer ever to win 11 LPGA tournaments. The next year, Annika joined only six others to complete an LPGA Career Grand Slam.

Her career was a record-breaking marathon. In 2003, she played in a men's PGA Tour, and by 2007, she had 72 official LPGA victories, ten major championships and 18 international tours. She was top on the LPGA money list.

However, her domestic life suffered. She divorced in 2005, and in 2007 doctors discovered major injuries in her spinal column. This great athlete has yet to regain her previous form, and she declared her intention to retire at the end of 2008.

The unmistakable swing of Annika Sörenstam in action during the first round of the 2003 Skins Game, at Trilogy Golf Club in La Qunita, California USA. Sörenstam won four Skins tournaments totalling US $175,000 in prize money.

Seen here in 2008, the year in which she announced her retirement, Annika Sörenstam holds the championship trophy after winning the Michelob Ultra Open at Kingsmill Resort and Spa, Virginia, USA.

Tiger Woods (1975 –)

Tiger Woods is a phenomenon. He was two years old when he started playing golf, and not yet three when he appeared on television putting against the movie-star golfer, Bob Hope. At the age of eight, he won the Junior World Golf Championships, and went on to win this six times. He was the youngest-ever winner of the US Junior Amateur championship. During the first peak of his professional career, startled golfing authorities began 'Tiger-proofing' their courses. They lengthened the yardage on the tees, hoping to hobble Tiger's chances and renew hopes of a win among his competitors.

Eldrick Tont Woods was born in Cypress, California on 30 December 1975. His family called him Tiger, and this is how the world knows him. His father, Earl, a US Army lieutenant colonel, was Tiger's golf mentor and teacher, but Tiger follows the Buddhist faith of his mother, Kultida. The golfer describes himself as an American who is 'Cablinasian', a word he coined to encapsulate the rich heritage from his Caucasian, Black, Native American and Asian forebears.

Tiger enrolled at Stanford University, but two years later, in 1996, he turned professional. In April 1997, he won The Masters, the youngest golfer ever to do so, and also the first black American to win. By the end of that year, Tiger had won three more PGA events, while setting a total of 20 Masters records and tying six others. A mere 42 weeks after he entered the professional ranks, he was Number One in the Official World Golf Rankings. Tiger's handsome appearance and captivating smile endeared him to all golf lovers, and contributed to his growing popularity as much as does his genius on the links.

A disappointed Tiger Woods misses a birdie putt on the 16th green, during the third round of the BMW Championship. This was the third event of the new PGA Tour Playoffs for the FedEx Cup at Cog Hill Golf and Country Club, Lemont, Illinois, USA, in 2007.

A very proud Earl and Kultida Woods with their young son Tiger, in September 1990.

Tiger Woods always pulls in the crowds. He is an enigmatic character as well as an incredible golfer. Here he hits his tee shot, watched by the spectators on the 17th hole, during the second day of the Tavistock Cup at the Isleworth Golf and Country Club, Windermere, Florida, USA, in 2006.

Tiger Woods (continued)

There was a slowdown in his game during 1998, a year in which he won only one PGA Tour event. Tiger explained to a mystified world that he was undertaking further coaching with Butch Harmon to improve his techniques. He returned in 1999, to dominate the world of golf by winning eight PGA Championships. He was voted Associated Press Athlete of the Year for the second time in three years, and was the PGA Tour Player of the Year.

During 2000, Tiger proved himself the supreme golfer when he broke or equalled many records. His victory margin in the US Open broke a record that had been set in 1862 by Old Tom Morris. He won the Triple Crown of Golf – the US, British and Canadian Opens – a feat previously achieved only by Lee Trevino. Tiger was also the youngest golfer to achieve the Career Grand Slam. His scoring average is the lowest level in PGA Tour history, and he was the first athlete to be named – for a second time – the *Sports Illustrated* Sportsman of the Year in 2000.

A smiling Tiger Woods poses with the trophy after winning the Target World Challenge at the Sherwood Country Club on 16 December 2007, at Thousand Oaks, California, USA.

Tiger Woods plays a bunker shot on the tenth hole during the final round of the 2008 Masters Tournament. In the same month Tiger underwent surgery on his left knee after suffering a torn ligament ten months previously.

In 2001, the golfing world had to take on board a new level in the game, the so-called Tiger Slam. The champion was the first ever to hold all four major championships at the same time. This remarkable success could not be officially recognised as a Grand Slam because the 12 months embracing his wins did not fit into a calendar year. However, he won the most PGA Tour wins in 2001 and also, for the fourth year running, he was named Player of the Year.

His game slowed in 2002, while 2003 and 2004 were not dazzling. Tiger suffered with an injured left knee that had to be surgically enhanced, and there was a rift with his coach, Butch Harman. He married in 2004 and his wedding was an elaborate ceremony, demanding time-consuming arrangements. His game fell below the high standard he set himself, and which the world had come to take for granted. He lost his Number 1 world ranking to Vijay Singh. Tiger then replaced his coach with Hank Haney.

Tiger Woods (continued)

Hitting a powerful shot, Tiger plays the 16th hole during the third round of the Tour Championship, the final event of the new PGA Tour Playoffs for the FedEx Cup at East Lake Golf Club, Atlanta, Georgia, USA, in 2007.

Tiger roared into 2005 to win, among other important tournaments, the Masters, the British Open Championship and six money events on the PGA Tour. He took the Number One position from Singh, lost it, regained it and then confirmed his superior status by winning the British Open.

Earl, his much-loved father, died in May 2006. Tiger took time off from his career as he grieved for the man who had given him so much support and confidence. When he returned to play for the 2006 US Open, his form did not initially show the old brilliance but his genius had not been extinguished – he won. In the British Open later that year, Tiger was leader in the field, playing a score that was only one stroke off the record he set in 2000.

His dominance in the game returned and during 2006 and 2007, Tiger won his 50th professional tournament, the youngest golfer to achieve this score. In his first 11 seasons, he surpassed career records set by Byron Nelson and Jack Nicklaus by notching up 51 wins in the PGA tour and a total record of 11 in major tournaments. He won the Jack Nicklaus, Byron Nelson and Arnold Palmer Awards, the highest honours given by the PGA Tour. He won the Tour Championship, the only golfer to win this twice, and found victory at the inaugural FedEx Cup. His overall scoring average gave him the lead over Phil Mickelson, Ernie Els, Justin Rose and Steve Stricker. The Associated Press named him – for a record-breaking fourth time – as the Associated Press Male Athlete of the Year.

However, the demands of his athletic life began to affect his health. The year 2008 started well with his 62nd win on the PGA Tour, and he was leader again at the World Golf Championships, among other spectacular victories. In April, he had further surgery on his left knee, but was ready for the US Open where his chief competitors were Phil Mickelson and Adam Scott. Tiger had to work hard to stay in the field, but by the fourth day he produced a birdie to win his 14th major championship. Tiger then confessed that, for the past ten months, he had been suffering from a torn ligament in his left knee and would have to withdraw from playing while he underwent surgery.

Although the golfing world and sports journalists were enthralled by Tiger's prowess, some noted that he had not excelled when playing in the Ryder Cup teams. But these doubts about his strengths as a team player are eclipsed by Tiger's supreme talent as a golfer. His is the lowest-ever career scoring average, and his earnings are the highest of any player in the history of PGA Tours.

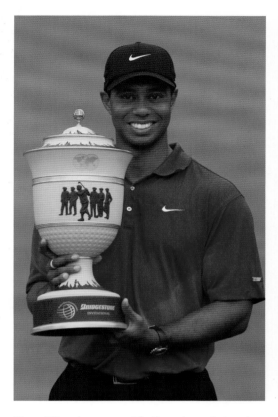

Tiger Woods poses with the winner's trophy at the WGC-Bridgestone Invitational, 5 August 2007, at Firestone Country Club in Akron, Ohio, USA. This was also the year that his daughter Sam was born.

For nine of his 12 years as a professional he has been top of the world rankings. He is the only player to win four major professionals without a break, and ranks with Jack Nicklaus in winning each major at least three times. In 2008, Tiger became the first to win the PGA Tour five times or more. He has had 65 PGA Tour wins and seven European Tour wins. And so on.

His remarkable golfing achievements are many, but Tiger bolsters his undoubted talent with a couple of superstitions. He always wears a red shirt during the final round of any tournament, and he has never abandoned the putter he first used in 1999. Using this, he has won 11 of his 12 majors. He has proved an astute businessman, starting with the endorsement contract he signed with Nike at the beginning of his professional career in 1996, and ever since, Tiger has earned millions in endorsements. As an 'ambassador' for Gillette, he has become a friend of his fellow 'ambassador', the tennis champion, Roger Federer.

His book *How I Play Golf* sold over a million copies with its first print run and in 1997, he appeared on the Oprah Winfrey show. Incidentally, this is where he used the word 'Cablinasian' to describe his racial heritage. In 1996, with his father, Tiger established the Tiger Woods Foundation and through this, he founded numerous charitable concerns to educate children and promote the game of golf. It has set up the Tiger Woods Foundation National Junior Golf Team to compete in the annual Junior World Golf Championship.

Tiger is involved in designing a number of golf courses around the world: the Ai Ruwaya golf course in Dubai; the Cliffs at High Carolina; and Punta Brava, at Ensenada in Mexico. He proved his skill in other fields when he won a charity motor race for the Steve Williams Foundation that brings sport to disabled children. Steve is Tiger's current caddie. In 2006, Tiger was awarded a place in the California Hall of Fame, and in 2007 he was inducted at the California Museum of History, Women and the Arts.

Tiger and his Swedish wife, Elin Nordegren, married in 2004 at the Sandy Lane resort on Barbados, and have a daughter who was born in 2007. They own properties in Wyoming, California, Florida and Sweden. However, in 2009, Tiger Woods' carefully cultivated personal image was a topic of much discussion in the press after allegations following an automobile accident near his Florida mansion.

This picture was taken in January 2008. It shows from left to right: Tiger Woods, Sam Alexis, Kultida Woods and Elin Nordegren, at the dedication of the statue honouring his father Earl Woods at the Tiger Woods Learning Center, Anaheim, California, USA.

Tiger Woods holds his daughter Sam, after winning the playoff round of the 108th U.S. Open, at the Torrey Pines Golf Course (South Course) on 16 June 2008 in San Diego, California, USA. Tiger claims that playing with his little girl is the best exercise for his injured knee!

Introduction

CHAMPIONSHIPS

The golf championships are a complicated and strange circus. Just when you thought that you knew your Ryder Cup from your Asian Tour, the FedEx Cup appears to complicate matters! Without trying to confuse you further, we have featured some of the major events that the best players in the world want to, or are invited to, attend.

These are often competitions that integrate with one another or may be a spin-off of another, but all the same they each have their own merit and their own unique character.

Join us at some of the world's biggest tournaments, from The Masters to the fledgling FedEx Cup, read about who won what and how it all came about. Hopefully, we can inspire you to follow one or more of these competitions to see what happens at close quarters.

US Open
The Masters
Ryder Cup
Solheim Cup
Presidents Cup
Walker Cup
PGA Tour
PGA European Tour
Asian Tour
LPGA Tour
FedEx Cup
World Golf Championships

US Open

In the late 1800s, there were enough golf enthusiasts in the United States to justify the formation of an association of clubs and players. The need for this became imperative in 1894. In this year, there was some confusion over two matches. One had been played at St Andrew's (New York) and the other at Newport, but no one was sure which should be recognised as the official amateur championship tournament, and there was no independent authority to make that decision.

In 1895, golfing club representatives gathered together. They came from Brookline (Boston), St Andrew's (New York), Newport (Rhode Island), Chicago (Illinois) and Shinnecock Hills (Long Island). The meeting became the Amateur Golf Association, later known as the United States Golf Association (USGA). A 36-hole competition played at Newport in October 1895 was the true beginning of the US Open. The game fielded amateurs and professionals, and was won by the Englishman, Horace Rawlins.

The US Open has become one of the Majors, as the four highest-prestige tournaments are called. The other three are The Masters, the British Open, and the PGA Championship. (Incidentally, the British Open is generally referred to simply as 'The Open'). If a golfer wins all four in one year, he has a Grand Slam. The US Open accepts qualifying professionals and amateurs, both men and women. It continues to be administered by the USGA, and the final round is always scheduled for the third Sunday in June, which is Father's Day in the USA.

Golf phenomenon Ben Hogan posing with the trophy after winning the US Open Golf Championship in 1948 at the Riviera Country Club, California, USA.

South African professional golfer Gary Player hits the ball on the fourteenth hole in front of spectators at the US Open golf tournament at Bellerive Country Club, St. Louis, Missouri, USA in June 1965.

The US Open has a well-structured qualifying process. Winners from the last ten years of the US Open are automatically included, as are those from the last five years of the other three major tournaments. There are exemption categories, and there is a qualifying system – the Local Qualifying in the US and the Sectional Qualifying, played in the USA, Europe and Japan.

This tournament is played annually at a different course each year, and the 72-hole game is set up to make high scores difficult, with a premium placed on accurate driving. A tight scoring system at, or around, under par by the leaders makes it hard for anyone to win by a wide margin. The course is longer than usual and has a high cut of rough. Those courses chosen as venues for the US Open often need re-modelling to meet tournament demands, and course designer Rees Jones specialises in these makeovers.

Jack Nicklaus tees off during the 1980 US Open at Baltusrol Golf Course, USA.

Seen here is the 411-yard, par 4, 18th hole, on the Black Course at Bethpage State Park, Farmingdale, New York, USA, the venue for the 2009 US Open.

For the first 15 years, the tournament was won by non-Americans. Winners came from England or Scotland. At last, in 1911, John J McDermott, a native-born American, was the winner. After that, Americans remained at the top, apart from in 1920 when Ted Ray from England was the champion.

The run of American wins remained unbroken until 1965, when the South African master, Gary Player, won the US Open. The next non-American champion was the Australian, David Graham, in 1981. It took another South African, Ernie Els, to break the American run again in 1994. Between 2004 and 2007, all the winners were non-Americans but the great American player, Tiger Woods, won the tournament in 2008.

This tournament is associated with grand performances from some of the best golfing heroes. The earliest and perhaps the best-loved champion is Bobby Jones. He played as an amateur in 11 tournaments, and for ten games he made the top ten. He won in 1923, 1926, 1929 and 1930. No wonder golfing fans were astonished and dismayed when this player retired at the youthful age of 28.

Ben Hogan had less luck when he started the tournaments, but after poor performances in his first four attempts, he made the top five in his next five matches. He won four times between 1948 and 1953. He also won three times in a row. Gene Sarazen won twice, as did Ernie Els, among about a dozen others. But the winners who have won the US Open four times are Willie Anderson, Bobby Jones, Ben Hogan and Jack Nicklaus. Hale Irwin, who had a reputation for beating tough courses, won three US Opens in 1974, 1979 and 1990. His last win made him the oldest champion at the age of 45 years.

Hale Irwin with the trophy during the 1990 US Open at Medinah Country Club, Medinah, Illinois, USA. Hale Irwin became the oldest US Open winner with a final score of 8 under par.

Tiger Woods sinks his birdie putt on the 18th green, to force a playoff with Rocco Mediate during the final round of the 108th US Open. This was held at the Torrey Pines Golf Course (South Course) on 15 June 2008 in San Diego, California.

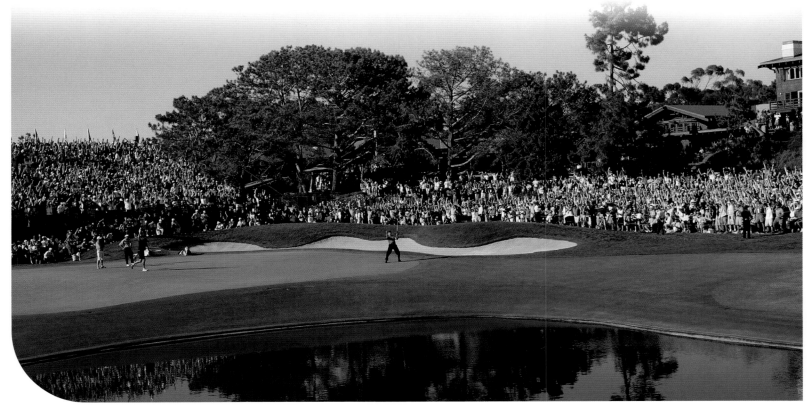

20 June 1994.
A victorious Ernie
Els hugs his caddie
Ricky Roberts after
winning a three way
playoff on Monday at
Oakmont Country
Club, Oakmont, USA.

Then there is Jack Nicklaus. He came in the top ten 18 times and was winner in 1967, in 1980 when he set a record, and in 1962 and 1972. He shares the record for the lowest 72-hole score in the Amateur wins and has the record for the lowest 18-hole score. He was one of the oldest players to make the US Open cut when he was 58. The youngest ever player, by the way, was Tadd Fujikawa of Hawaii, who was 15 years old when he qualified for the tournament.

Tiger Woods has made his mark on the US Open. His first successes were in 2000 and 2002. He won again in 2008 after a sudden death play-off against Rocco Mediate. This win has made Tiger only the sixth player to win three or more US Opens. These figures indicate the challenge that the US Open offers to even the greatest golfers.

This tournament has been played at clubs across the United States. Oakland Hills Country Club in Bloomfield Hills, Michigan, has hosted it a number of times, as has Oakmont Country Club in Pennsylvania. For fans, it adds to the excitement of the game, because each different, tough course allows the possibility of unpredictable shows of superb golfing.

15 year old qualifier, Tadd Fujikawa from Hawaii, hits a tee shot during the Monday practice round for the 2006 US Open Championship at Winged Foot Golf Club, on 12 June 2006 in Mamaroneck, New York, USA.

Champion Tiger Woods and Rocco Mediate, runner up, share a moment of camaraderie on the 18th green during the trophy presentation after the playoff round of the 108th US Open. This was held at the Torrey Pines Golf Course (South Course) on 16 June 2008 in San Diego, California, USA.

The varying choice of venue also gives all the states a chance to host this special tournament, delighting local golfers. The Northwood Club in Dallas and the Hazeltine National Golf Club in Chaska, Minnesota have had their turn, but it is the important role of the US Open in the Majors that makes this a popular tournament, drawing millions of television viewers.

Tiger Woods kisses the trophy after winning on the first sudden death playoff hole, during the playoff round of the 108th US Open on 16 June 2008.

The Masters

The Masters holds a special place in the game. The tournament, which was founded by a favourite golfing hero, is always held in the Augusta National Golf Club. It has a scenic, beautiful course and the Club has some arcane traditions, together giving the tournament a special atmosphere.

In 1931, Bobby Jones, the great amateur champion, with his friend, Clifford Roberts, purchased a farm in Augusta, Georgia. Here, Bobby planned a course with the designer Alister MacKenzie. The Augusta National Golf Club was born and ready for the players in 1933; Mackenzie died before the first tournament was held in 1934.

There was some disagreement over the naming of the event. Bobby preferred the name Augusta National Invitation Tournament to The Masters, a title he thought pretentious. But The Masters stuck and was soon in common usage, and in 1939 became the official title.

The Masters is one of the four major championships in men's professional golf. In 2003, Martha Burk staged a protest against this male-only rule, demanding a ladies' tournament, but the Augusta National Golf Club did not relent. The event is a 72-hole tournament held over four days in April every year, set so that the final day falls on the second Sunday of the month. It abides by the rules of the United States Golf Association, augmented by special regulations of the Club.

Seve Ballesteros of Spain acknowledges the crowd on the 18th hole during the final round of the US Masters, played at the Augusta National Golf Club, USA.

Gary Player of South Africa drives off the 15th tee during practice for the 2006 Masters.

Groups play in a set of three players for the first 36 holes, played over the opening Thursday and Friday. A cut is then made, and on Saturday and Sunday, the winners play for the championship. In deference to its founder, Bobby Jones, amateurs are invited to play The Masters. They are drawn from the winners of the most prestigious amateur tournaments in the world.

For the first two days, the defending Masters Champion is paired with the current US Amateur Champion. Since 1952, the Club has presented a Silver Trophy to the lowest score made after the cut by an amateur, and a few years later, started awarding a Silver Medal to the amateur runner-up. The Club houses amateur players, who are presumed to be less well-off, accommodating them in an extension to the clubhouse known as the Bird's Nest. The young amateur, Tiger Woods, stayed here in 1995. He was also the only amateur to make the cut that year.

The Augusta National Golf Club is a wealthy institution, and prides itself on its traditions. Since 1949, the Club has honoured the winning player with a green jacket, the same as that worn by Club members. This jacket signifies that the champion is now an Honorary Member of the Club. He can keep it for a year, then it is stored at the Club for him to wear whenever he visits. It is now part of the winning ritual for the previous winner to put the green jacket on the new winner. Gary Player, for some reason, refused to store his jacket at the Club but claims he has never worn it except in the Club grounds.

The jacket is not the only award. The Club honours the winner with a Gold Medal, while his name is engraved on the championship Silver Trophy. The Club keeps this trophy, but it does give the champion a replica to take with him to keep. For five years after his win, the champion automatically receives an invitation to play in the other three major tours, and earns a lifetime invitation to The Masters, among other Club privileges awarded to him.

The runners-up are not neglected. In 1951, a Silver Medal became part of the ritual, and in 1978, the Club added a Silver Salver for the runner-up.

Phil Mickelson helps Zach Johnson put on the green jacket as Masters Chairman Billy Payne stands at the podium during the ceremony, after Johnson had won the 2007 Masters Tournament.

Then there is the Champions' Dinner, held on the Tuesday before the tournament starts. Guests are members of the so-called Master Club, all past winners of The Masters. Selected members of the Augusta National Golf Club are given honorary status, and the defending champion selects the menu. Ian Woosnam, the Welsh winner in 1991, asked for lamb wrapped in hay and slowly roasted, a traditional dish from his native country.

Often, The Masters starts with an honorary opening tee shot at the first hole. Those chosen are champion veterans of the game. Between 1963 and 1972, Jock Hutchison and Fred McLeod together did the honours. Hutchison retired because of ill-health, so McLeod teed off alone in 1973 and repeated the performance until his death in 1976. The Club did not immediately replace these great players.

Worthy replacements were found in 1981, when Gene Sarazen and Byron Nelson played the opening shots. Sam Snead joined them in 1984. In 1999, Sarazen died and Nelson retired in 2001. Snead continued until 1999 but died in 2000. Again, the Augusta National Golf Club did not hurry to replace these heroes, then Arnold Palmer was invited to make the opening tee shot in 2007 and 2008.

Honorary starter Arnold Palmer hits his first tee shot to mark the start of the 2008 Masters Tournament.

Caddies were selected by the Club and, until 1982, were always African American. Now players can bring their own caddie, who must don the Club attire of white jumpsuit, green cap and white tennis shoes. The name of the player is marked on the back of the caddie's jacket. The defending champion's caddie is always No 1; other numbers are drawn in the order of the players' registration for the event.

The Club makes awards not related to the PGA Tour. It honours players for particular achievements. The Daily Low Score wins the Crystal Vase; a Hole-in-One gets the Large Crystal Bowl as does a Double Eagle. An Eagle earns the Pair of Crystal Goblets and a Par 3 winner receives a Crystal Bowl.

The Masters was suspended in World War II during the years 1943–1945. The Club raised cattle and turkeys on the greens as part of the war effort. Later, the tournament became very exciting in the 1960s and '70s when Arnold Palmer, Gary Player and Jack Nicklaus competed in titanic struggles. Television brought millions of fans the delight of being able to follow some, if not all, of the game.

The Augusta National Golf Club has jealously guarded the tournament and its greens from the rampages of television cameramen, and has made some complicated arrangements with the networks. Commercial interruptions are tightly controlled, and broadcasters who show ignorance of the correct golfing terms or those who are ill-mannered are given short shrift. Overseas coverage is also carefully controlled and licensed. The Club is fortunate in that money from sponsors is of little importance to its financial affairs. It can afford to stipulate its regulations for, and its expectations of, public and media alike.

Phil Mickelson watches his daughter Amanda miss a putt on the ninth green, alongside his other daughter Sophia, during the Par-3 contest prior to the start of the 2007 Masters Championship.

British golfer Sandy Lyle taking his shot during the US Masters golf tournament in 1988. Lyle went on to win the event.

View of a famous green blazer in the clubhouse locker room at the Augusta National Golf Club, USA.

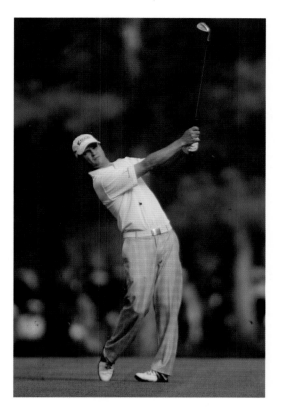

Zach Johnson plays a shot during the final round of the 2008 Masters Tournament.

Leader Trevor Immelman of South Africa blasts out of the sand on the second hole during the final round of the 2008 US Masters.

Radio broadcasts have not proved as complex a problem, and since 1956, Westwood One has given ball-to-ball coverage on every tournament. The BBC has radio broadcasting rights, and agreements have been made with Irish radio.

The public are welcomed but demand is high and tickets, although not expensive, are difficult to obtain. Applications for practice rounds need to be made a year in advance and are chosen by random ballot. Tickets for the tournament are restricted to members of a patrons' list, but this may be closed for years while the Club works through all the applicants. The list was extended in 2008 to include children aged between eight and 16 if they were accompanied by a patron.

The 1980s Masters are remembered for the bad luck and disappointments suffered by Greg Norman. Again and again, he lost the championship by a whisker. For instance, in 1987 a sudden-death play-off was lost to Lary Miza, not a golfer known on the world stage. Greg hit a birdie and lost on a winning tie against Jack Nicklaus. But this was also the era that saw non-American players emerge, with winners Seve Ballesteros of Spain (1983), Sandy Lyle of Scotland (1988) and Nick Faldo of England (1989), among others.

The Masters was electrified by the arrival of 21-year-old Tiger Woods in 1997, when he broke a four-day scoring record that had stood for over 30 years. Vijay Singh from Fiji won in 2000, but the following year, Tiger completed his 'Tiger Slam' when he won The Masters, his fourth straight major championship win in one year. In 2002, he was the third player to win The Masters over consecutive years. Phil Mickelson won in 2004 and 2006, but Tiger Woods carried off the trophy and the green blazer for the fourth time in 2005. Zach Johnson was the 2007 winner and The Masters champion for 2008 was Trevor Immelman.

The greens are heated when they are in shade, and the preparation and cutting of the course meets the highest standards. Various grasses have been tested and the main course is now covered with bentgrass, a narrow blade that has speeded up the putting surfaces; as a result, some of the contours of the green have had to be flattened. The sand in the bunkers is white feldspar. Every hole on the course carries the name of a plant; for example, one is called Dogweed!

Trevor Immelman of South Africa celebrates winning the 2008 Masters Tournament.

Trevor Immelman has a green jacket placed on him by Zach Johnson after winning the 2008 Tournament.

The course has been altered over the years, and of course the changes have attracted criticism. Gary Player approved the latest changes made in 2006, during which the course was lengthened considerably, and his praise helped calm fans and players. The Masters remains a highly popular tournament, attracting television viewers as much by the beauty of the course, bordered by splendid azalea blooms, as by the competitors' golf form.

A scenic view of the azaleas on the eighteenth hole, at the Augusta National course, during the 2006 Masters Championship. Seen here is Phil Mickelson of the US on the eighteenth hole, during the third round play on the Sunday morning.

Ryder Cup

British and American professional golfers met to compete in a friendly game in 1921, and met again in 1926. On both occasions, there were suggestions that, perhaps, the tournament could be formalised into a regular event. A British player in the 1926 game listened to the chatter. Samuel Ryder was not only an enthusiastic golfer but also a wealthy man, and he decided he would found and fund a formal tournament. He donated a cup and even agreed to pay prize fees to members of the winning team.

The first Ryder Cup match took place in 1927 at the Worcester Country Club in Massachusetts, and it was agreed that the tournament would be played every two years. This timetable was suspended during World War II, and altered after the 9/11 attacks in September, 2001. In deference to this tragedy, the Ryder Cup was moved to 2002 and ever since then has been played every even-numbered year. The original rules were for a US team to play a combined British/Irish team; in 1979 this was altered to expand the British/Irish team into a European one.

Samuel Ryder, the donor of the Ryder Cup, presents the trophy to winning captain George Duncan of Great Britain, after they had beaten the USA in 1929 at Moortown, Leeds, England.

The European team player Ian Poulter celebrates with the trophy after Europe's victory over the USA at the 35th Ryder Cup Matches. These were held at the Oakland Hills Country Club, on 19 September 2004 in Bloomfield Township, Michigan, USA.

Other changes meant that the Ryder Cup came to be played over three days instead of two, and the number and pattern of games has evolved. It moved from a total of 12 matches to 24, and then to 32 matches. However, in 1979 this was changed to a 28-match format and this number still applies.

The Ryder Cup match is now jointly administered by the PGA European Tour and the US PGA. The tournament takes place over three days, Friday through to Sunday, and each team comprises 12 players. Methods of selecting teams differ between the two authorities. The Americans have a complicated system that gives points on prize money earned at selected tournaments. The European team is selected from players on the European Tour and the world ranking points list. The tournament is held alternately in the US and Europe.

On both Friday and Saturday, there are four foursome matches between two teams of two golfers. Each player on the same team takes alternate shots throughout the match, using the same ball. The winning team is measured by the lowest combined score for each hole. On these days there is also a four-ball match. Again, two teams, each with two golfers, play but they use their own ball, and the win depends on the lowest score of an individual team player. The game on Sunday is a singles match, the standard matchplay competition between two golfers. The captains, often previous champions who are now non-players, are free to use their team members in any combination over the three days of the Ryder Cup.

The par 5 18th hole at Valhalla Golf Club, in Louisville, Kentucky, USA, the venue for the 2008 Ryder Cup Matches.

Ryder Cup team members carry great status, confirming the importance of the tournament for golf lovers all over the world. Players regard inclusion in the Ryder Cup team as an important part of their professional career, although not all the great players are good at playing as part of a group.

European Team Captain Ian Woosnam kisses The Ryder Cup Trophy during the closing ceremony, after Europe had won by a score of 18¹/₂ – 9¹/₂ on the final day of the 2006 Ryder Cup at The K Club in Straffan, Co. Kildare, Eire.

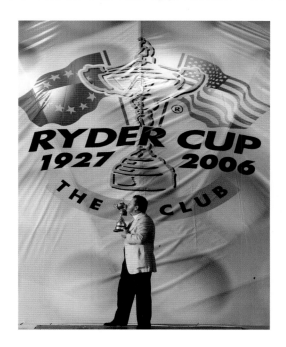

This tournament has become one of the most exciting events on the golfing calendar. Of course, there have been unpleasant spats between European and American players, although these are rare, and recently, matches have been marred by rowdy displays of nationalism from the gallery. The tournament crowd reduced the Ryder to a 'bear pit', according to one European captain. The Americans, in turn, complained of exhibitionism and gamesmanship from the European team. However, both the American and European PGA are working to control the galleries and to restore the manners and friendly spirit associated with the game of golf.

European captain Nick Faldo of England and US captain Paul Azinger joke around at the previews for the 2008 Ryder Cup, held at Valhalla Golf Club on 22 October 2007 in Louisville, Kentucky. The US team were ultimately victorious in their quest to win the 2008 Ryder Cup.

Solheim Cup

This tournament is as important to women golfers as the Ryder Cup is to male competitors. Its administrators are well aware of the significance of both events to golf fans. For instance, the Solheim used to be played in every even-dated year, but when the Ryder postponed their tournament after 9/11, Solheim changed to fit in with the men's altered schedule. The Ryder Cup became an even-numbered year event and the Solheim played on odd-numbered years.

Karsten Solheim, the Norwegian-American golf club manufacturer for whom the cup is named, was significant in setting up this tournament. Basing it closely on the structure devised by the Ryder Cup, the first event was held at the Lake Nona Golf and Country Club in Orlando, Florida. The inaugural year was 1990, and the Cup was taken by the USA under the captaincy of Kathy Whitworth.

The victorious US team with the cup, after clinching a thrilling win in the 2005 Solheim Cup, at Crooked Stick Golf Club, on 11 September 2005 in Carmel, Indiana, USA.

The victorious American team celebrate after winning the 2002 Junior Solheim Cup matches between USA and Europe, held at the Oakridge Golf Club in Edina, Minnesota, USA on 18 September.

SOLHEIM CUP | **GOLF**

USA captain Patty Sheehan holds the trophy above her head after winning the 2002 Solheim Cup between USA and Europe. This was held at the Interlachen Golf Club in Edina, Minnesota, USA on 22 September.

Solheim Cup (continued)

The format is the same as for the Ryder Cup. This means it is run over three days and comprises eight foursomes, eight four-balls and 12 singles. (Please see the Ryder Cup entry for a full explanation.) Team selection is not quite the same as it is for the men's tournament and, of course, the rules for the format have shifted and changed over the years. Since 2007, the European team comes from the top players of the LET and four are selected from the Women's World Golf Rankings. Invariably, European players play the majority of their competitions on the LPGA Tour, so the golf rankings are important to the European Solheim selectors. The captain is allowed to choose some players – 'the captain's pick'. The Americans select their teams from the LPGA lists.

The Solheim Cup is significant for the players. For instance, Annika Sörenstam, a major champion in women's golf, was pleased to be selected and made an important contribution to the tour. The captains are frequently chosen from retired players, and they are selected for their experience, steadiness and leadership qualities. All these captains have played in the Solheim Cup, and include Patty Sheehan, Mickey Walker, who was captain four times, and Nancy Lopez. Between 1990 and 2007, the Americans won nine times, and the Europeans five times.

Louise Friberg of Team Europe follows through on a shot during an exhibition four-ball match against Team USA, at the preview event for the 2009 Solheim Cup. This was held at Rich Harvest Farms golf course on 14 July 2008 in Sugar Grove, Illinois, USA.

Venues for the Solheim Cup have ranged across the US, Britain and Europe: in the US, Virginia, Indiana and Minnesota; in Europe, Wales, Scotland, Ireland and Sweden.

In 2002, the PING Junior Solheim Cup was inaugurated. It was designed for junior amateurs. The girls, 12 in each team, are chosen in the USA from the American Junior Golf Association. On the other side of the Atlantic, selectors in the UK and Europe choose from similar associations. The format is different from the Solheim: the tour takes place over two, not three, days, although the girls play six foursomes, six four-balls and 12 singles. The venue is one as close to the Solheim Cup course as possible. This Junior Cup serves an important role in enthusing girls and young women about the glorious game, whether as amateurs or future professionals.

The Lexus Cup is another major tournament for women and this pits an Asian team against a so-called international team from nations outside Asia. It follows the Solheim format.

Linda Wessberg of the European Team hits her second shot on the 10th hole during the afternoon four-ball matches of the 2007 Solheim Cup, held at the Halmstad Golf Club in Sweden on 15 September.

Presidents Cup

Retief Goosen of South Africa hits out of the sand on the 18th hole during Saturday afternoon's Four-Ball matches at Royal Montreal Golf Club, host of the 2007 Presidents Cup on 29 September, in Canada.

The Presidents' Cup was established as a tournament where non-European players could prove their game on the world stage. It was devised by the Americans; the opposing team was to be non-Americans and non-Europeans. They were to be known as the International team: generally, the players come from the Southern Hemisphere.

The first tournament was held in 1994 at the Robert Trent Golf Club. The Americans were captained by Hale Irwin and his team emerged victorious. In 1996, Arnie Palmer led the second American winning team. At last, in 1998, when the venue was the Royal Melbourne Golf Club in Australia, the International team won the tour. Ken Venturi was the captain.

There is not a long history to this tournament, but already a dramatic legend has been established. This occurred at the 2003 Presidents Cup when the teams met at The Links, Fancourt Hotel and Country Club in George, South Africa. This course, by the way, has a magnificent setting. The tour was anticipated with much excitement, for both teams were fielding terrific players. The Internationals were captained by Gary Player and the Americans were led, again, by Arnie Palmer.

As the tournament drew to its close, the teams were tied by regulation at 17 points. The scores demanded a sudden death play-off in three holes. The players were two giants, Tiger Woods for the US and Ernie Els for the Internationals. Characteristically for the area, the sun was falling rapidly and still there was no resolution. Captains Gary and Arnie found a solution: they agreed that the teams should share the Cup, thus confirming the true spirit of golf.

The American team is selected from the list of official earnings, and the Internationals are selected from the Official World Golf Rankings, but players from the European Ryder Cup teams are debarred. Each team has 12 members, two of whom are selected by the captain. It is a biennial event.

The distinctive flavour of this Cup arises from its honourable intent to create a global tournament and widen the appeal of golf. Its purpose is emphasised by the special status of the Honorary Chairman, who is chosen from the national leaders of the American and the non-European participating countries. This, of course, accounts for its title, The Presidents' Cup. In 1994, then-President Gerald Ford held the position for the first Presidents' Cup. Former president George Bush and his son, former president George W Bush, have both been Honorary Chairmen. Bill Clinton held the position in 2000, but the Australian Prime Minister, John Howard, had the honour in 1998, and Thabo Mbeki of South Africa was chosen in 2003.

Players do not earn any money from the Presidents' Cup. Each player in the winning team is awarded prize money, but this is then donated to a charity of the captain's and the team's choice. The first six tournaments have raised 13 million dollars and this has been distributed on a world-wide basis to a variety of charities. This system symbolises the worthy reasons behind the founding of The Presidents' Cup.

For three of the tournaments, The Presidents' Cup has been held at the Robert Trent Jones Golf Club, named, of course, in memory of the famous champion, Bobby Jones. However, the venue is not fixed, and since both South Africa and Australia have hosted the event, it is likely that fans may follow the real game in their country – if it fits the 'international' definition.

International Team player Adam Scott playing on the second hole during the Foursome Matches of the Presidents' Cup 2007.

K J Choi of the International team plays a bunker shot on the third hole, during the final day of the singles matches at the 2007 Presidents' Cup in Canada.

Mike Weir of the International team and Tiger Woods of the US team pose with the Presidents' Cup trophy on the first tee during the fifth round of the singles competition for the Cup on 30 September 2007.

Mike Weir of Canada teeing off on the third hole during the final day's singles matches at the Presidents Cup 2007.

Walker Cup

This is a major amateur tournament bringing together teams from the US and Great Britain with one from Ireland. It began as a conversation with delegates who met at St Andrew's in Scotland. The world was making a slow recovery after World War I, and the golfers gathered to discuss golfing rules and etiquette. Chat passed to regular matches, and the 1895 champion amateur and then president of the USGA, George Herbert Walker, offered to donate the cup to a formal tournament.

George Herbert Walker was the grandfather of the former American president, George Bush Snr, and great-grandfather of former president George W Bush. Both men inherited Mr Walker's great love of the game and are keen amateur players.

The press dubbed the tournament the Walker Cup at its first competition, held in 1922 at the National Golf Links of America at Southampton, New York State. The American team were the first winners. For many years, the American team dominated the Walker Cup, but recently the British/Irish team have evened out the number of wins.

Pictured on 7 May 1930, at the Surrey Golf Club, England, the American Walker Cup team take a break during practice. The team included Bobby Jones, second from the left.

28 May 1971: The jubilant British golf team (back - left to right) Humphreys, Foster, Bonallack (captain), Marsh, Green, Stuart and Carr, (front) Marks, MacDonald and MacGregor, with the Walker Cup on the St Andrews Golf Course after their victory over the United States.

Oliver Fisher of England birdies on the 16th hole during the afternoon singles matches in the 2005 Walker Cup Match on 13 August. The Chicago Golf Club in Wheaton, Illinois, USA was the venue.

Walker Cup (continued)

The Walker Cup started as an annual event but after 1924 became a biennial event, played initially every even-numbered year. It altered after World War II to follow odd-numbered years. The venues alternate between American and British or Irish courses, and the Walker Cup has been played in some of the most beautiful courses on both sides of the Atlantic. The Chicago Golf Club has hosted the event twice; in 2007 it took place in the Royal County Down Golf Club in Ireland and, of course, the Walker Cup has been played most often (six times) at St Andrews in Scotland.

The US team is selected by the US Golf Association, while the British and Irish players are chosen by the Royal and Ancient Club of St Andrews. Each association selects ten players and a captain. Unlike the Ryder Cup, the Walker has not embraced European golfers.

The format for the Walker Cup is four games of foursomes over 18 holes each morning, and eight singles in the afternoons. The tournament is played over two days. Incidentally, the Ryder Cup followed this format for a short period but that competition, designed for professionals, inevitably changed to a more complex pattern.

The victorious American team with the Walker Cup (L-R kneeling) Jonathan Moore, Billy Horschell, Rickie Fowler, Colt Knost, (L-R standing) Chris Kirk, Dustin Johnson, Kyle Stanley, Buddy Marucci (captain), Webb Simpson, Jamie Lovemark and Trip Kuehne at the end of the 2007 Walker Cup Matches. This was held on the links of the Royal County Down Golf Club on 9 September in Newcastle, Northern Ireland.

There has been some spectacular golf played by the amateurs who have competed at the Walker Cup. Perhaps the most memorable is the 1995 game when the veteran Gary Wolstenholme beat the 20-year-old prodigy, Tiger Woods, on the first day. The youngest player to join the tour is Oliver Fisher who was just under 17 years of age in the 2005 Cup.

The great Bobby Jones captained the US team in 1928 and 1930, leading his players to victory on both occasions. During a long run of US wins between 1932 and 1949, the Americans were led every time by Francis Ouimet. In 1999, 2001 and 2003, the British won every tournament and Peter McEvoy was captain for two of those games. In 2007, Buddy Marucci was captain of the winning US side, and Colin Dalgliesh captained the British side; both these men were named as captains of their teams for the 2009 Walker Cup, played at the Merion Golf Club in the United States.

The Walker Cup brings a glamour and prestige to amateurs equal to any professional tour, and offers hope to a huge number of golfers that they may prove their ambitions and reveal their skill at the game.

Jonathan Moore, left, of USA celebrates with his teammates after putting for an eagle to retain the Walker Cup for the USA, during the final day of the 2007 match against Great Britain and Ireland.

Great Britain and Ireland golfer Rhys Davies hits out of the 18th bunker during the final day of the 2007 Walker Cup Match against the USA.

Golf had a hesitant start in the New World even though it was first advertised in a 1779 New York magazine as 'this pleasant and healthy exercise'. It was much later, in the 1880s, that golf began to gain popularity, leading to a building spree of club courses and public links. Some control of game rules was required, and in 1894 the Amateur Golf Association was formed to 'assure orderly control of the game'. This evolved into the United States Golfing Association to administer the Amateurs, Opens and Women's tournaments and the Public Links in America. It remains the US authority on golf rules and etiquette, and is responsible for solving disputes.

Walter Hagen did more than anyone to break down the barriers between amateurs and professionals, and was determined to widen the golf-playing population. In 1916, Walter, with a group of his fellow professionals, laid plans for a Professional Golf Association Championship. They were encouraged by Rodman Wanamaker, the son of a Philadelphian department store magnate. He offered a trophy and $2,580 prize money for a PGA champion event. The first President of the PGA was Robert Harlow, who had been Hagen's manager.

Two greats of American golf: Walter Hagen, on the right, with Jim Barnes during the 1920s.

American Chez Reavie celebrates after winning the RBC Canadian Open at the Glen Abbey Golf Club on 27 July 2008 in Oakville, Ontario, Canada.

The first PGA tour opened on 10 October 1916 at the Siwanoy Country Club, Bronxville, New York State. A match-play tournament, it was won by Long Jim Barnes. Members intended the PGA to be an annual event, but the championship was suspended during World War I. It was resumed in 1919 and, again, Long Jim won the match. Walter Hagen was the 1921 champion, then Gene Sarazen had his turn in 1922 and 1923; Hagen then won every tournament between 1924 and 1927.

Professional golfers were beginning to make serious money, particularly when Fred Corcoran took over the management of the PGA. He held this position from 1937 to 1947. Huge monetary advances were made under his care, confirming the glamour and importance of the PGA Championship. Fans were delighted when in 1952 the Cup was carried off by Jim Turnesa. He was one of seven golfing brothers, but victory at a PGA Championship had eluded every single one of them until Jim's winning game.

Parker McLachlin hits off the 18th tee during the final round of the Legends Reno-Tahoe Open at the Montreux Golf & Country Club on 3 August 2008 in Nevada, USA.

Garrett Willis chips onto the fifth green during the final round of the 2008 Wyndham Championship at Sedgefield Country Club in Greensboro, North Carolina, USA.

In 1958, the format was changed to stroke-play and the first winner under this regime was Dow Finsterwold. The event was televised and drew a huge audience, greatly enhancing the popularity of golf. The Wanamaker Cup became a coveted award among professionals who play by invitation.

Thrilling records have been set during the years of this major tournament. In 1935 Gene Sarazen hit 'the shot that was heard around the world' when he hit an albatross (or double-eagle) on the par 15th hole, forcing a play-off. Sarazen won by five strokes the next day. In 1963, the Par 3 Contest was begun and in 1962, Gary Player, a South African, won the Cup. Jack Nicklaus won it four times between 1963 and 1980, and when he was 46 years old, he won again in 1986. Gary Player was to win it twice.

Tiger Woods took the tournament by storm. His win at Medina Country Club, Illinois, in 1999 was thrillingly close. In 2000, he had a major battle against Bob May, scoring the first ever 3-hole aggregate, and was the first to equal the three major championship wins in one year set by Ben Hogan in 1953. Tiger won again in 2000, 2006 and 2007.

The PGA Championship is now one of the world's great sporting events, attracting fans and viewers from beyond golf. The skill of the players, the tension of the game and the sums of money involved capture the general imagination. As with all PGA Tours, this Championship raises millions of dollars for charities.

Padraig Harrington of Ireland celebrates with his wife Caroline, his two children, his caddie Ronan Flood, and the PGA Championship Trophy. This was following his win at the 90th PGA Championship at Oakland Hills Country Club on 10 August 2008 in Bloomfield Township, Michigan, USA.

PGA European Tour

The golf tour system has a muddled history. It started as a vague brotherhood of clubs and small associations but, as money assumed an important role in the game, so formal structures developed. The more powerful groups devised a system in which a 'tour' would encompass a series of tournaments; winners would be assessed by their tournament scores and the financial gains they made. The number of finalists on a tour is controlled by a 'cut', meaning that those competitors who have the worst scores halfway through the series are dropped from the tour.

The PGA European Tour reveals a typically wayward past. It began in Scotland where, in 1860, The Open Championship was staged for professionals, but so few played that it was later opened to amateurs. In 1901, The Professional Golfers' Association, representing the British and European players, approved the Open Championships, although the tournaments continued to be organised by clubs or sponsors. This did not help the golfers' incomes, which remained low even after the advent of television coverage.

The US had introduced a structured tour system in the 1930s, and this did benefit American golfers. The Professional Golfers' Association did not adopt the system until 1972, when they introduced the PGA European Tour. Initially, the season ran for six months, and the 20 tournaments were played generally in Great Britain, although European venues were accepted and there was even an event held in Tunisia. In 1984, The Professional Golfers' Association handed the administration over to an independent PGA European Tour organisation, and the headquarters are based at the Wentworth Club in Virginia Water, England.

9 March 2008: Arjun Atwal of India in action during the final round of the Maybank Malaysian Open, held at the Kota Permai Golf & Country Club in Kuala Lumpur, Malaysia.

Martin Kaymer of Germany hits his second shot on the 17th hole during the final round of the Abu Dhabi Golf Championship at Abu Dhabi Golf Club on 20 January 2008.

The PGA European Tour has assumed a global reach, having played as far afield as Dubai and Bangkok, but prize money is still considerably lower than on the PGA Tour. The administrators added the Volvo Bonus Pool, giving extra prize money to winners, and in 1998 started increasing individual tournament prizes, the so-called European Tour Order of Merit. They added the three US Majors – the US Open, the PGA Championship and The Masters – to their series schedule.

The European Tour is second only to the PGA Tour in status among golf's tours, and was used to attract outstanding players from Commonwealth countries. However, as the US grants sporting scholarships to young players, a practice forbidden in Britain and Europe, contemporary young players tend to bypass the European Tour and head for America.

Spanish golfer Miguel Angel Jiménez celebrates after getting a hole-in-one at the 5th during the final round of the BMW PGA Championship on the West Course at Wentworth, England, on 25 May 2008.

Pablo Larrazabal of Spain poses with the trophy after winning the Open de France ALSTOM, at the Le Golf National Golf Club on 29 June 2008 in Versailles, France.

Money motivates them. The European Tour demands 11 tournaments to qualify as a winner; because the Tour now schedules so many other tours, a player only needs to play four of the European Tour series. Then, the player can add in 6 entries on other tours on the schedule to qualify, and in this way, earn more on US schedules. It is estimated that the European PGA Tour's financial resources are about 50% of the PGA Tour.

Recently, South African, Australian, Chinese and Asian tournaments have been included in the Tour, and The Race to Dubai 2009 tournament will replace the Order of Merit. This should increase the coffers of the European PGA Tour.

The European PGA Tour lasts over the 52 weeks of a calendar year with a break for the Christmas season, and runs to 50 tournaments. The Spaniard Miguel Angel Jiménez won in 2008. Other champions include Ernie Els of South Africa who won from 2001 to 2004, his run broken in 2005 by Colin Montgomerie of Scotland. Colin himself had a run of unbroken victories between 1995 to 1999. In the '70s and '80s, Peter Oosterhuis of England, Seve Ballesteros of Spain, and Sandy Lyle of Scotland dominated the lists.

Mikael Lundberg of Sweden in action on the 18th green, during the final round of the Inteco Russian Open Championship at the Moscow Country Club on 27 July 2008.

Asian Tour

The Asian Tour was established in 1995, an extension of the successful PGA structure devised to advance the professional game. There are over 20 tours run by a PGA or sometimes an independent organisation. Tours were devised to create a pinnacle championship between winners of a series of tournaments; a tour is justified in a geographical region where there are an adequate number of established tournaments to fulfil a series.

The rudiments of the system started with the founding of the PGA of America in 1916, and were extended in 1932 when the then-manager, Bob Harlow, established a 'playing pros' prize money structure. Records of the players' earnings, the 'money list', were opened in 1934, and have been maintained ever since. A formal recognition of the tours system was made in 1968 when the Tournament Players Division split from the PGA of America, and the players themselves took control of the PGA Tours.

Gonzalo Fernandez Castaño of Spain chases a peacock away during a practice round of the EMAAR - MGF Indian Masters at Delhi Golf Club on 5 February 2008 in Delhi, India.

As the popularity of golf spread, serious enthusiasts emerged from countries where the game was a comparatively new sport. Despite being 'transplanted', there were enough players, clubs and associations to make golf an important sport in the daily life of these countries.

The Asian circuit developed in this way and as the countries in this region grew wealthier, and assimilated modernity into their cultures, local professional golfers looked to increase their incomes. They wanted of course to be part of the world golf stage. Sponsors and broadcasters, too, longed to be part of a successful, wealthy sport. Asia wanted to raise its game status from a golf circuit to a golf tour.

The PGA Tour, following their policy of widening their arena, helped open the Japan Tour in 1973 and a southern African tour called the Sunshine Tour. In 2007, the International Federation of PGA Tours listed six full members: the PGA Tour, in the US; the European Tour, with series in Africa, Asia and Australasia; the Japan Golf Tour; the Sunshine Tour, and the Asian Tour. (Obviously, Japan was not included in the Asian Tour when that was established in 1995.)

The usual PGA rules apply to these 'developmental' tours. On each tour, the player-members are those who have played in most of the tour's series of tournament events. This earns them a 'tour card'. There are entry tournaments, called the 'Q-School' or Qualifying School, although some players are invited due to their golfing achievements elsewhere. Player-members pay entry fees and travel costs, which are forfeited by those who lose in the cut.

SSP Chowrasia of India celebrates with the trophy after winning the final round of the Emaar-MGF Indian Masters 2008.

Malaysian golfer Ben Leong poses with the trophy after winning the Worldwide Selangor Masters at Petaling Jaya on 9 August 2008. Leong won the championship to take home US$48,147 in prize money.

The Asian Tour has proved to be highly successful. In 1990, The Japan Golf Tour was third in the financial hierarchy, but in 2007 it had fallen below the Asian Tour which was then listed fifth. This reflects changes in the global economy, but also shows the major cultural and political advances that have taken place in India, Korea, Malaysia, China and other Asian countries.

The Indians have proved keen players, and to date, six Asian Tour champions have come from this country. SSP Chowrasia, who won the Indian Masters of 2008, is the newest hopeful, but stars also include Mardan Mamat of Singapore and Hendrik Buhrmann of South Africa, who won the Amby Valley Asian Masters in 2006. The Steel Authority of India sponsors the SAIL Open, one of the four tournaments in the Tour series; Greg Norman designed the magnificent course, the Jaypee Greens in Delhi, India. The PGA Asian Tour is the only officially recognized pan-Asian golf tour and its players qualify for World Ranking status.

A victorious Padraig Harrington, seen here during the 2008 PGA Championship after making a par putt on the 18th hole, during Sunday play at Oakland Hills CC., Bloomfield Hills, USA.

LPGA Tour

The Ladies Professional Golf Association was formed in 1950 by a group of American professional women players. It embraces not only Tour players, but club professionals and coaches. In this it differs from the PGA Tour, their male counterpart, which is exclusively for tour professionals. The PGA of America controls all amateurs, male coaches, clubs, public links and also the rules of play.

Although most LPGA Tours are held in the USA, the Association has a structure similar to the PGA Tour system and shares its ambitions in popularising golf around the world. In this aim the LPGA has been singularly successful. Through the Ladies' European Tour, the LPGA co-sanctions the Women's British Open, the French Evian Masters, the Korea Championship and the Mizuno Classic in Japan, which includes tournaments in China. 2008 saw three tournaments in Mexico and one each in Canada, Britain, France, Japan, Singapore, China and South Korea.

Se Ri Pak of Team Asia poses for a photo with the trophy after winning the Lexus Cup 2007 at The Vines Resort & Country Club in Perth, Australia.

Annika Sörenstam, left, of Sweden is presented with the 2005 LPGA Vare Trophy by LPGA Commissioner Carolyn Bivins, during the awards reception, held at the Mar-a-Lago Club, West Palm Beach, Florida, USA on 18 November 2005.

The LPGA has its headquarters in Daytona Beach, Florida, USA, and throughout its history has fought hard for women professionals to earn high fees in prize money. It has attracted major sponsorships, and only women tennis players equal the sums earned by professional women golfers. The LPGA Tour holds a series of weekly tournaments between the months of February and December, and prize money in 2008 exceeded US $58 million.

The annual major championships held under the auspices of the LPGA are the Kraft Nabisco Championship; McDonald's US LPGA Championship, sponsored by Coca-Cola; the US Women's Open; and the Ricoh Women's British Open, held in co-operation with the Ladies' European Tour. Following the PGA structure, women golfers play initially through an annual Q-School (Qualifying School) and top players qualify for the next year's Tour.

Lorena Ochoa of Mexico is held aloft by close family members in the water beside the 18th green, after winning the 2008 Kraft Nabisco Championship at the Mission Hills Country Club, Rancho Mirage, California, USA.

Three annual awards judged on a competitive basis are given by the LPGA. The Vare Trophy, named for Glenna Collett-Vare, is given to the player with the lowest scoring average for the season. This trophy carries great prestige. The Rolex Player of the Year trophy uses a complicated formula to assess the winning recipient. Then there is the Louise Suggs Rolex Rookie of the Year award, named after a founding member of the LPGA. This is awarded to a first-year player on the Tour, and is given to the player who scores the highest through a changing number of points for tournaments and wins. The Association makes numerous other awards.

In the early years of the LPGA Tour, American players dominated. From 1953 to 1965, the Vare Trophy was awarded to Americans, and from 1966 until 1995 the Player of the Year award went to Americans. But since 2000, there have been 28 non-American winners, drawn from Sweden, Great Britain, Canada, Korea, Australia, Germany and Taiwan. The US may have lost its domination but the list of recent players shows the triumph of the LPGA's ambition to spread the global popularity of golf.

For many years, from the late '80s until 2005, the Swedish player Annika Sörenstam dominated the LPGA Tour. She was Player of the Year 12 times and won the Vare Trophy six times during this period. With Karrie Owen in competition, she has been top money winner for over a decade. The Mexican player Lorena Ochoa finally broke Annika's seemingly invincible position. Lorena was the Player of the Year and received the Vare Trophy in 2006 and 2007.

Earlier champions have won enduring fame through their wins. These include Betsy King, Nancy Lopez, Beth Daniels, Mickey Wright and the inimitable Kathy Whitworth, who was the Player of the Year eight times during the 1960s.

Yani Tseng of Taiwan holds the trophy after winning the McDonald's LPGA Championship at Bulle Rock Golf Course on 8 June 2008, in Havre de Grace, Maryland, USA.

In-Kyung Kim of South Korea completes her final round at the 18th hole during the 2008 US Women's Open Championship held at The Interlachen Country Club, in Edina, Minnesota, USA.

Natalie Gulbis of the USA hits her second shot, at the 2nd hole, during the final round of the 2008 Ricoh Women's British Open Championship held on the Old Course at Sunningdale Golf Club, England.

FedEx Cup

In 2007, a new trophy appeared in the world of professional golf. It was advertised as 'the first ever' PGA Tour play-off for the FedEx Cup. The final venue was at the East Lake Golf Club in Atlanta. This Cup seemed an excellent addition to the PGA Tour list, adding a second rung of 'majors'. The sponsors talked about millions of dollars in prize money, but Tiger Woods chose not to play in the first tournament and fans were asked to consider the reasons behind his decision.

FedEx mounted a powerful and intense promotion. They moved beyond the usual caps, shirts, memorabilia and images. Three thousand employees in the Atlanta area were ordered to wear hats bearing the FedEx logo; any parcels delivered in the Atlanta area for two weeks prior to the event were to be decorated with FedEx logos; trucks in New York were wrapped in FedEx Cup advertisements. Radio and TV broadcasters were required to mention the event frequently. Fans could enter a sweepstake or practise golf against a specially constructed 'golf hole wall' in Manhattan, among other things.

Steve Stricker poses with the trophy after winning the 2007 Barclays tournament with a sixteen under par. This was the inaugural event of the new PGA Tour Playoffs for the FedEx Cup and was held at the Westchester Country Club, in Harrison, New York, USA.

Tiger Woods, seen at East Lake Golf Club in Atlanta, Georgia, USA, holding the FedEx Cup trophy following the final round of the 2007 Tour Championship, which is the final event of the new PGA Tour Playoffs for the FedEx Cup.

It seemed the advertising gurus had forgotten the concept of overkill. Perhaps, too, they sadly neglected the spirit of golf. Wright Thompson, Senior Writer at ESPN magazine and ESPN.com, expressed his anger and concern. He described golf as 'a languid sport. It is one of small, personal glories.' Yes, golf is not a team game; you can play by yourself, you can share anecdotes and swap your victories with those of your club's members. Fans are not focused on a team because they admire the individual achievements of the player.

It is understood that golfers have an unwritten code of honourable respect towards the game of each individual player. This 'code' permeates the game at every level from golfers in small country clubs to the great heroes of the game. This is why expressions of nationalism displayed by the gallery at the Ryder Club have been found offensive.

A FedEx truck decorated with the FedEx Cup trophy is displayed during the first round of the Northern Trust Open, held on 14 February 2008 at Riviera Country Club in Pacific Palisades, California, USA.

Wright Thompson resented FedEx's grandiose claims to be an 'historic' event. He wrote that the FedEx Cup 'seems actually to believe that greatness is simply the result of a marketing campaign and not something that develops over time.' He continued, 'The PGA Tour took its own idea and then, out of insecurity or idiocy, seriously damaged it with a marketing/promotion campaign.' Thompson observed that the heavy coverage first irritated, then bored, the fans.

Tiger Woods, seen here in action, taking a drive from the tee during the 2007 FedEx Cup.

South African Rory Sabbatini taking a shot from the rough at the 2007 Deutsche Bank Championship for the FedEx Cup at TPC Boston, Norton, Massachusetts, USA.

Fans like their golf to hold unexpected flashes of brilliance, the display of true athleticism; they nurture memories of great moments in world tours but also those of a buddy at their local green. Are these the things the world's greatest golfer, Tiger Woods, pondered before deciding that he wouldn't be playing in the opener of the Tour?

What form did the FedEx Cup show in 2007? The tournaments started at Barclays in New York, moved to the Deutsche Bank Competition in Boston, thirdly to the BMW Competition in Chicago, then Greensboro and finally, East Lake. The points were reset in the play-offs. One blogger, Bill Ratledge, pointed out that if the PGA was serious, it should have required all qualifiers to play in every event. Under the FedEx system a one-point lead was the same as a 1000-point lead. Others observed that it spoiled the majors, extending the season when TV viewers were geared to the football season, and asked, was it just a vulgar money-making ploy?

Tiger Woods won, despite avoiding the Barclays tournament. It was his 61st win. Arnie Palmer won 62 victories during his career. Is this what inspired Tiger? After all, he didn't actually need the 1.2 million dollar win. Some fans regretted his ambitions, others hailed his game. It is yet to be shown whether golfers and enthusiasts alike need or admire this FedEx Cup Tour.

World Golf Championships

The structures and systems of the professional golf game are truly byzantine in their complexity of lists, titles and prizes. Naturally, the wealthier the administrators and players become, the more varied and complicated are the ways of increasing their income. The commercial followers, or hangers-on, have grown into an army of sponsorship and promotional deals. In fact, the latest twist represented by the FedEx Cup stirred fans and players to some rude observations about greed.

The PGA Tour became the International Federation of PGA Tours in 1996. The early aims of the first PGA of America, formed way back in the 1930s, were to improve the earnings of professionals and to spread the love of golf around the world. The players formed a Tours Players' Division in 1968 to control the tour system that had developed in the game. Leaving the PGA of America to guard the rules and the amateurs, their grouping was known as the PGA Tour, and this brought in sponsors. Television coverage helped to raise the prize winnings to astronomical levels, and Tour winners were able to increase these earnings with sponsorship deals.

Tiger Woods hits his tee shot on the 22nd hole during the 2008 Championship match of the WGC-Accenture Match Play Championship. The venue is The Gallery Golf Club, Dove Mountain in Marana, Arizona, USA.

David Duval tees off at the eighth hole, during the fourth round of play at the 2000 Andersen World Match Play Championships at La Costa Resort and Spa in Carlsbad, California, USA. Duval beat Scott Hoch five and four, saying that the round confirmed that his game was finally beginning to get back to the shape it was earlier in the previous year.

World Golf Championships

Golf became a game that appealed to sportsmen of all nations, and the PGA Tour sanctioned tournaments and tours in Europe, Africa and Asia. They formed the International Federation of PGA Tours, and more and more events cluttered golfing calendars everywhere. The World Golf Championships were part of this growth. Member tours of the Federation are the Asian Tour, the European Tour, the Japan Golf Tour, the PGA Tour, the PGA Tour of Australasia and the Sunshine Tour in southern Africa. The LPGA was not involved.

This Federation also agreed on a structure for a world-wide ranking system and shared control of sanctions for significant competitions, including those at a world level. The World Golf Championships were born. To inaugurate this new competition, three tournaments were chosen. These were the Accenture Match Play Championship, the Bridgestone Invitational and the CA Championship. Formats vary with match play, stroke and team. Individuals win the tournaments, but two players representing their country play the World Golf Championship. A strong field was guaranteed by the selection system. Although players come from winners in events in many countries, and the World Golf Championship has been played in five continents, the golfers have generally been listed in the Official World Golf Ranking. Prize money exceeds one million dollars.

Geoff Ogilvy holds the winner's trophy after the completion of his final round of the WGC-CA Championship held on 24 March 2008 on the Blue Course at Doral Golf Resort and Spa in Miami, Florida, USA.

250

GOLF | CHAMPIONSHIPS

In the debut tournaments in 1999, Jeff Maggert won the first and Tiger Woods won the remaining two. At the World Cup held in Argentina in 2000, the American team of Tiger and David Duval won the trophy. At this point sporting calendars in the US were suspended after the 9/11 attack.

The Americans, with Tiger, won again in 2003 but in 2004, the South African duo, Ernie Els and Retief Goosen, were World Golf Champions. The Americans, with Tiger Woods playing, have proved the dominant winners of this Tour. Tiger has won the singles six times in this Championship Tour, a record number in one particular tournament.

The World Golf Championships donate proceeds to the charity, The First Tee. This promotes the provision of access to golf for the impaired and those in financial need. The Championship helped launch First Tee chapters in Spain and Canada. It has achieved the ambition of spreading golf abroad, and the World Golf Championships symbolise international unity. They provide a stage for the national heroes to prove themselves, thus giving fans in every nation a stake in the game.

Vijay Singh of Fiji poses with the Gary Player Cup after winning the 2008 World Golf Championships-Bridgestone Invitational. The Championship was held on the South Course at Firestone Country Club, Akron, Ohio, USA.

Index

Index (cont.)

Acknowledgements

The Publisher and authors would like to thank the following people and organisations for their kind help and contribution:

Lilleshall Hall Golf Club for allowing us to use their facilities.

The Westin Turnberry Resort, Scotland : 124,125(T),125(B)

Getty Images

Adrian Dennis/AFP: 125; Allsport Hulton/Archive: 153; Andrew Redington: 124,134 – 135,203,213,215(T),232(L); Andrew Redington/Allsport: 105,116; Andy Lyons: 219, 242(L); Andy Lyons/Getty Images for Golfweek) :210,211(T); Augusta National: 88,89(TR),86 – 87; Barry Iverson//Time Life Pictures: 135(RI); Bill Stahl/Pictorial Parade: 195; Bob Martin/Sports Illustrated: 89(BL),211(B); Bob Thomas:152,156,170,178,207; Brian Morgan: 90,161,169,202; Central Press: 174,224(L); ChrisCondon: 182,251(L),192 – 193; Chris Condon/US PGA TOUR: 222(I),245(B); Darren Carroll: 113; David Alexander: 98,99(T),99(B),104,121, 146,147(T),147(B); David Boily/AFP: 220; David Cannon: 96,97,100,106,107,108,110,111,117,118,119,126, 127,128,129,132,133,138,140,141,142,143,148,157,168,171,179,196,214,215(B),216(T),216(B),217,225,226(I) ,232,237,241,242(R),243; David Cannon /Allsport: 120,130,131,112,149,175; Donald Miralle: 249; Doug Pensinger: 201(T),201(B); Eric Schweikardt/Sports Illustrated: 173; Evening Standard 158; Fred Vuich /Sports Illustrated: 239,101,103,246; General Photographic Agency: 228; Glyn Kirk/AFP: 233; Hans Knopf/Pix Inc./Time Life Pictures: 194; Harry How: 115,187,206,209(T); Haynes Archive/Popperfoto: 212; Hulton Archive: 166,177; Hunter Martin: 181; Ian Walton: 235; Jacqueline Duvoisin/Sports Illustrated: 91(T),91(B),199; James Drake/Sports Illustrated: 159; Jamie Squire: 204; Jeff Gross: 198(B); Jim Gund/Sports Illustrated: 208; John Dominis//Time Life Pictures: 176; John G. Zimmerman/Sports Illustrated: 94,95,160; John Kelly: 197; Jonathan Ferrey: 218; Ken Levine: 183; Kevin C. Cox: 230(R); Lester Cohen: 190; Louis Van Oeyen/Western Reserve Historical Society: 165; M. Ehrmann: 244; Marc Feldman: 155; Max Morse: 230(L); Mike Ehrmann/Sports Illustrated: 247; New York Times Co.: 172; Nick Wilson: 139; Paul Kane: 240(R); Peter Muhly/AFP: 226 – 227,227(I); PGA Tour Photo Services/PGA): 198(T); Popperfoto: 163,164,224(R); Richard Heathcote: 154,200; Rick Stewart: 92,93; Robert Laberge: 186,229; Ross Kinnaird 232(R); S.Greenwood: 188,245(T); Scott Halleran: 184,221(BL),240(L),248,150 – 151; Sean Garnsworthy/ALLSPORT: 136,137; Simon Bruty /Allsport: 102; Stan Badz: 250; Steve Grayson/WireImage: 180; STR/AFP: 238; Streeter Lecka: 222 – 223; Stuart Franklin: 189,236,251(R); Tim Sloan/AFP: 209(B); Timothy A Clary/AFP: 205,221(TR); Topical Press Agency: 162; Travis Lindquist: 191; Warren Little: 109,114,144,145,234; Yale Joel/Time & Life Pictures: 167; Front Cover: Getty Images/ Travis Lindquist

Special photography courtesy of Mirco De Cet.